Woman as 'Nobody'
and the Novels of Fanny Burney

Woman as 'Nobody'
and
the Novels
of Fanny Burney

Joanne Cutting-Gray

University Press of Florida
Gainesville Tallahassee Tampa Boca Raton
Pensacola Orlando Miami Jacksonville

AA26792

Copyright 1992 by the Board of Regents of the State of Florida.
Printed in the United States of America on acid-free paper.

Cutting-Gray, Joanne.
    Woman as 'Nobody' and the novels of Fanny Burney /
Joanne Cutting-Gray
        p.   cm.
    Includes bibliographical references and index.
    ISBN 0-8130-1106-X (acid-free paper)
    1. Burney, Fanny, 1752–1840—Criticism and interpretation.
2. Women and literature—Great Britain—History—18th
century. 3. Alienation (Social psychology) in literature.
4. Feminism and literature—Great Britain.   I. Title.
PR3316.A4Z586   1992
823'.6—dc20   91-22254
                                                              CIP

The University Press of Florida is the scholarly publishing
agency for the State University System of Florida, comprised of
Florida A&M University, Florida Atlantic University, Florida
International University, Florida State University, University of
Central Florida, University of Florida, University of North
Florida, University of South Florida, University of West Florida.

Orders for books published by member presses should be
addressed to
University Press of Florida
15 Northwest 15th Street
Gainesville, FL 32611

For my daughters, Jennie and Julie.

Contents

Acknowledgments

A PREPARATORY STUDY of chapter 1 is printed as "Writing Innocence: Fanny Burney's *Evelina*," *Tulsa Studies in Women's Literature* 9:1 (Spring 1990): 43–57. I am grateful to the editors for allowing me to draw on this study. Everyone who reads Burney and writes about her is indebted to her editors, especially Joyce Hemlow; to her biographers, in particular, Margaret Doody; to both her pioneering and recent critics, Patricia Meyer Spacks, Mary Poovey, Kristina Straub, and Julia Epstein. I am personally indebted to the following persons who read this manuscript in various stages: Claudia Johnson, Ed Duffy, Al Rivero, Michael Gillespie at Marquette University; the editors and readers at the University Press of Florida; Karen Ford and James Swearingen for invaluable advice and encouragement.

Introduction

I'm Nobody! Who are you?
Are you—Nobody—Too?
Then there's a pair of us?
Don't tell! they'd advertise—you know!

How dreary—to be—Somebody!
How public—like a Frog—
To tell one's name—the livelong June—
To an admiring Bog!
                    —Emily Dickinson

ENGLISH NOVELIST FRANCES BURNEY (1752–1840) claims to have been
fifteen years old when she began her earliest diary (1768–1778).[1] In
the first entry of that journal she wonders with whom she will converse. She imagines herself "talking to the most intimate of friends,"
but an imaginary friend whom she calls "Nobody," since "to Nobody
can I be wholly unreserved—to Nobody can I reveal every thought,
every wish of my heart, with the most unlimited confidence, the
most unremitting sincerity to the end of my Life." Later in a still
girlish hand, she adds the superscription, "This strange medley of
Thoughts & Facts was written at the age of 15. for my Genuine &
most private amusement." Signed, "Fanny Burney."

When Burney says that "I must imagine myself to be talking—
talking to the most intimate of friends," she implies that there are
prior conditions for friendly converse. To be "wholly unreserved,"
to reveal "every thought" with "unlimited confidence" and "unremitting sincerity" calls for trust and openness, a real dialogue that
for most women of her time could only occur in private. She invites
a reply by asking Nobody to imagine her as a friend, as somebody
worthy of attention. As the only reader of her diary, she herself
becomes the nobody to whom she writes, a person without substance.
In the act of inventing "Nobody" she opens up a conversation with
the "unknown, unnamed" and names her own alterity.

"Why, permit me to ask, must a *female* be made Nobody?" In that single poignant question Burney defines the inevitable problem for one who inhabits the dominant culture as an outsider. In light of her frequent disclaimers of authority, there is more than verbal gesture in that phrase, "permit me to ask." Why does she need permission? From whom does she profess to seek legitimation? And why must a female be made—both forced and fabricated—to be Nobody?

Read from the vantage point of twentieth-century gender studies, the truth for Burney is that she does not exist, except as the other of a discourse from which she is excluded. Though mutually determined, Woman and Man are not equal entities in a cultural hierarchy that has long considered the former a "negative, corrupt, undesirable version of . . . [Man,] a fall away from it."[2] Yet Burney doesn't treat herself as the woman constructed by patriarchy; instead, she lets Nobody function as the alterity, the *unnamed* feminine that determines the structure of identity for man, the named. When Burney dismantles this opposition in her ongoing dialogue, she shows us that Woman-as-Nobody springs out of a difference that has the configuration of Somebody-as-Man. In terms of gender, this strategy enables Burney to use the conceptual vocabulary of the patriarchy without being a party to it. By using "Woman" as a conceptual name and "Nobody" as woman's place in culture, Burney imaginatively shapes herself out of the "strange medley" of an unfinished life. Her address, therefore, speaks to the heart of our concern with gender.

Burney-as-Nobody asks questions requiring that both she and her audience give themselves to the play of dialogue. If conversation means engagement, then she cautions "Miss Nobody" against the disengagement of reading as a "stranger," a resistant, detached observer: "If any stranger was to think it worth reading, how capricious—insolent & whimsical I must appear!" She adds, "no matter! It's [sic] truth & simplicity are its sole recommendation" (1769). Writing between friends allows for "undisguised thoughts," frees her from the consistency of a fixed identity. When another friend, Mary Ann Waddington, once complained that the letters Fanny wrote were too short, Burney replied that "the basis of Letters, as of Friendship, must be KINDNESS, which does not count lines and words but expression and meaning." Instead of making veridical assertions, conversational writing opens a space for a community of friends. Burney wishes to understand Nobody-somebody-myself-community by thinking and understanding others.

Although Nobody names her status as a writer in a social context, writing enables her to accommodate those inhibiting structures that most tax her. Like Dickinson's poem about Nobody, Burney's address suggests a unique dignity and legitimacy reserved for those who remain Nobodies in a world of self-inflating somebodies. Even as she resists the patriarchal sense of identity, Burney continues to write narratives about female nobodies and shows us how both to dismantle and renovate Woman. Her problem and ours is identity as the named and difference as the nameless, a paradox of personhood implied in the two-in-one of dialogue.

This passage from the diary sets Fanny Burney's achievement as a writer in a very different light from that in which either her contemporaries or posterity have seen her. As she continues over a span of seventy-two years to write voluminously—diaries, novels, journals, pamphlets, letters, memoirs—she records both the brillance and eccentricities of the society in which she was more than a nobody. Prior to the rise of feminism, critics confined her powers to the domestic and modest. In a period of great formal invention— Fielding's comic epic in prose, Richardson's writing to the moment, Sterne's discontinuous narratives—her work was credited with literary charm. She was praised for depicting the life and manners of a world in which overwrought heroines, lacking experience, found their innocence threatened. Though thwarted by social entanglements, her proper heroines endured their female difficulties and were rewarded with marriage. Only recently have we begun to see that Burney's contribution to the rise of the genre was as great as, though different from, that of her older male contemporaries.

Feminism has enabled us to see the novels as a testimony to the way women have been poorly served by a male-dominated culture. Such a revisionist reading questions the traditional understanding of female propriety by inverting it. Rather than learning prudence, Burney's heroines, we are told, need to challenge the "proper" and create a more self-assertive identity. In other words, innocence and passivity become ideological negations that make females minus-males and precipitate all their difficulties.

While these two positions, traditional and revisionist, imply opposing views about gender, they actually share the same model of subjectivity, and hence, of woman. Both views mask a desire to be

the Subject and articulate the other subject as nobody. A modern
concern over the unarticulated forces inhabiting the blank spaces
and margins that Woman occupies suggests another way out of our
female difficulties and the either-or of those opposing views. What
had once been seen as narrative weaknesses in Burney's writing can
now be understood as an experimental project that avoids the mutual
determination of patriarchy and anti-patriarchy. Narrative gaps open
in her works when the female characters, unable to name according
to the language of the patriarchy that names them, must resort to
sickness, madness, or fits of hysteria in order to be heard, that is,
to become nameable. Crises occur for the heroine because the world
requires of her innocence, selflessness, and silence while simultaneously requiring that she respond decisively to concrete situations.

Although the later journals no longer question Miss Nobody, the
novels that follow interrogate the social practices that conceive Woman as mere negation. Namelessness and identity become Burney's
lifelong concern. What begins in a sprightly tone of friendly interrogation erupts at a crucial point in each novel as barely controlled
hysteria. Not only do her heroines seek for a legitimating patronym
to lend them substance, they also search for the naming power that
can speak for their unnamed experience. In the chapters that follow
we will read the name of Woman-as-Nobody in order to recapture
the experience within it. Burney's strategy of moving between somebody and nobody, the antinomies of male and female, will enable
us to distinguish between the various functions of nobody in the
social world and the persons who embody them.

In Burney's first and only epistolary novel, *Evelina* (1778), a retiring
young woman, nameless because unacknowledged by her father,
ventures into the social world for the first time. Under the watchful
eyes of her peers, Evelina seems a whimsical pawn in a world that
equates name with legitimacy and the tangible, patronym and
wealth. A patronym would protect her innocence; wealth, her social
standing. But lack of both name and voice turns her into a cipher.

The mode of narration makes this conventional narrative even
more problematic. Chapter one of this study, "*Evelina:* Writing Between Experience and Innocence," explores how the narrated Evelina
conceals her sexual and verbal power from herself and from others.
Why does the Evelina who writes with such acute observation and
wit, who names situations so as to deflate pretension and vulgarity,

seem so inept in the social world, especially in the company of young males? In a social situation where she must assume the disguise of innocence, Evelina becomes a problem to herself. When a crisis occurs over the use of her name, she writes to Lord Orville and discovers the power of naming that she has concealed from herself. Her writing, like Burney's diary, oscillates between public and private, opening a space for a new sense of identity, a name other than private nobody and public innocent.

In the next two novels, *Cecilia* (1782) and *Camilla* (1796), Burney abandons the epistolary form of *Evelina* and the *Diary* for the third-person omniscient narrative of classical Reason. Under the titles "*Cecilia:* The Madness of Reason" and "*Camilla:* The Heart Has Its Reasons," the second and third chapters will examine the relationship between namelessness and name in a context where to act is to be rational. Cecilia and Camilla, oppositional female characters, both use hysterical outbursts to disavow the discourse that names and silences them. As controlling authority of Reason, the narrative voice causes their language to register as hysterical, irrational, and mad.

When we learn that Cecilia, an orphaned heiress, can only obtain patrilineal inheritance if her husband takes her name and renounces his own, we are confronted again with the problem of namelessness and name. The three patriarchal guardians who are to protect her actually contradict her wishes, hiding their designs behind their reasons. Yet Cecilia, the most reasonable character in the novel, one who faithfully follows her inner dictates for "doing right," appears to all others as irrational and mad. The central scene describes a "just and reasonable" Cecilia harassed by the kind of reasoning based on prejudice and desire. Thus persecuted, Cecilia escapes into the irrational and goes mad.

Camilla offers a version of woman determined by eighteenth-century sentiment whose "feelings are all her virtues." Encouraged to live up to her identity as the female of "melting sensibility," Camilla's capriciousness delights her family. Why then, when she flirts or plays coy, acting according to the whimsical name they accord her, is she harshly judged? The calculating Edgar who wishes to marry her, for example, determines to test her constancy even as he insists that what most delights him is her inconsistency. Nearly as whimsical as Camilla, he conceives of himself as all prudence and considers his spying behavior rational even when he rages with jealousy. Camilla's uncritical belief that she is a creature of sentiment causes her to collapse in hysteria over the injunction against explaining her own behavior to him. Her feelings prevent her from seeing sensibility as utter calculation.

The mad scenes in these narratives, more horrifying than Evelina's barely controlled hysteria, create a disjunction between writing as a process of discovery and the already-written. Since the irrational has no name, no essential linguistic designation other than nonreason, Woman stands in for what reason cannot know and cannot name. In other words, the narrative fissures created by the intrusion of madness allow an opening for the females to name, to articulate suffering, mood, and sensibility.

Can the irrational be more reasonable than the reckoning misinterpreted as the rational? As Foucault has explained and Burney describes, the excluded discourse of madness actually determines reason. Camilla and Cecilia cry out against this exclusion, when they learn that their culture has misinterpreted them and so misnamed them.

Chapter four, "*The Wanderer:* Naming Woman," traces how Burney's growing concern with female namelessness becomes explicit in her last novel (1814). The story, set against the backdrop of the French Revolution, describes the secretive actions of a woman who refuses to reveal her purposes or real name to a rigid society. While the earlier novels concealed the name of woman under a dialectical exchange between silence and the irrational, this novel describes a woman, "Incognita," who *refuses* to name herself. Incognita, "unnamed, unknown," appears helpless and passive when persecuted by old dowagers and rapacious men, yet she pushes the rational discourse of a disintegrating patriarchy to the brink of hysteria.

What is so puzzling is that Incognita, wanderer of the title, is under no legal or rational constraint to keep her name (Lady Juliet Granville) a secret. She insists that her name, the status of her being, belongs to her husband, even though no laws would recognize the legitimacy of her forced marriage to a French official. Why does she refuse to name herself and thus end her female difficulties? She could adopt the self-disclosure of Elinor and become a resistant individualist, but instead she explores another possibility that transforms female personhood. She renames passivity and innocence, not as their opposites, but as forces complicitous with any agenda that liberates by opposition. Thus, Burney succeeds in describing a view of woman that eludes both the name imposed upon her by the old social order and the absolute freedom proposed by the new.

Chapter five, "'Nobody' Is the Author," returns to the early diary: "To Nobody, then, will I write my Journal." By the time we reach *The Wanderer*, a playful figure of speech has become a philosophical thesis about the identity of woman. That figure marks the shift in how language and identity relate to the play of difference. The traditional notion of woman's identity offered Burney only two options, outside or inside, identity or difference. But when, as in her diary, alterity (Nobody) is recognized as inhabiting identity (Fanny Burney), it becomes possible to step away from the opposition and move freely without mediation between identity and difference, somebody and nobody. Since "A Certain Miss Nobody" is also the author of the diary, Burney dismantles the notion of author as an original source or an individual preceding a text. "Nobody" replaces "author," and converts the entity "Fanny Burney" into a multivoiced community. Thus, Nobody is neither historical personage, Frances D'Arblay, nor author Frances Burney, but a conversational invention that produces subjectivity between the various names.

The closing chapter, "Woman's Revelation and Women's Revolution," places Burney's view of Woman alongside those of Kristeva, Lyotard, Arendt, and Irigaray. When Burney describes "Incognita" as "unknown, unnamed, without any sort of recommendation," she nearly repeats word for word a phrase she applied to Nobody in the early diary and to herself as editor of *Evelina*.[3] In those prefatory comments to *Evelina*, she disingenuously begs the reading public not to judge her as an "author," nor to compare her work to that of Johnson, Richardson, Smollett, and Fielding. She even describes the "humble Novelist" as occupying "inferior rank" in the republic of letters. She hastens to add that as "editor," "wraped" in "impenetrable obscurity," aware of the "imperfections" of the "letters," yet "trembling for their success," she fears "not being involved in their disgrace." Her appeal to the "magistrates and censors" of the "Monthly and Critical Reviews" implies that their names for authority are not consistent with her own. Even as published author, she does not try to confer an absolute authority as patriarchal censorship and authorial privilege control language.

The "unknown, unnamed" calls attention to the relation between writing, that is, naming as revealing, and the prohibition against speaking. Julia L. Epstein describes Burney's discourse as "imprisoned . . . by a disembodied primal language, a language both unutterable and ineradicably embedded in her imagination, clamoring for attention and shattering silence."[4] That primal language, understood as a process of revealing, is no longer a linguistic marker that points to named entities. The unnamed moment of possibility, the closet which Burney occupies as writer, editor, friend, is a space of discovery, a questioning *with* as well as *about* subjects. Accordingly, her female nobodies localize a feminist critique without either theorizing oppression out of existence or inverting the essentialism of patriarchy. Rather than writing the history of gender oppression, her works enact ways of living with gender differences.[5] Speaking between various nobodies and somebodies, Burney weaves herself as a figure in the warp and woof of letters, journals, and scraps. The strange medley is an animated conversation of many voices that delivers her from silence.[6]

1

Evelina: *Writing Between Experience and Innocence*

Thus ought a chaste and virtuous woman . . . lock up her very words and set a guard upon her lips, especially in the company of strangers, since there is nothing which sooner discovers the qualities and conditions of a woman than her discourse.

—Plutarch

A WORLDLY WISE, often subversive, journalist-narrator who represents herself as an inexperienced young rustic has intrigued, if not puzzled, the readers of Burney's first novel, *Evelina*.[1] The fact that Evelina's innocence can only be seen from the narrator's perspective beyond innocence, that innocence is a reductive concept within the broader, reflexive context of writing is an important clue to the quixotic conduct of Burney's first heroine. If, as T. B. Macaulay notes, "novel" was a name that produced shudders from respectable people so that a novelist sometimes risked social ostracism, then a female novelist, much like her fictional counterpart, risked even more.[2] It is no wonder then, that young Burney, single, genteel, and shy, kept her authorship a secret. No one, except perhaps her father, was more astonished than she at the immediate popularity of *Evelina*.

Aside from its popular reception, Burney's first novel also charmed the arbiters of eighteenth-century taste—Johnson, Reynolds, Burke, and Sheridan—and delighted Mrs. Thrale and Lady Mary Montagu. Mrs. Thrale, relieved to discover that *Evelina* was not "mere sentimental business," commented that "it's writ by somebody that knows *the top and the bottom,* the *highest* and *lowest* of mankind."[3] Early reviewers of *Evelina* praised its charming, unaffected glimpse into the social life of London, its satire of class and individual character, and its broad humor and pathos even as they cited its contrived plot and flatly conceived heroine as instances of its conventionality.[4]

9

Modern commentary, however, is more likely to laud *Evelina*'s publication in 1778 as a frontier: "Behind it are centuries of silence; in front of it, that 'damned mob of scribbling women' who seized upon the novel as a means of subsistence and self-expression and thereby challenged the masculine perspective that had previously dominated literature."[5]

As circumspect forerunner of what was called that "mob of scribbling women," Burney explained the innocent character of Evelina to her sister Susan by saying that she "had been brought up in the strictest retirement, that she knew nothing of the world, and only acted from the impulses of Nature."[6] Quoting from her own preface, she added that the heroine was the "offspring of Nature in her simplest attire." Though Evelina incarnates artlessness in a world of duplicity and evil, she nonetheless requires "observation and experience" to make her "fit for the world." Evelina under the guardianship of the Reverend Mr. Villars is the innocent in a private world of innocence until she sallies forth into a disjunctive, public world where, affronted by male assertiveness, she, as female, becomes a problem to herself. Unless one hears in Evelina's discourse a misguided effort to maintain the "simplest attire" of innocence, one will too often see only female compliancy. As long as she insists upon preserving her innocence-passivity (a symbol for the stasis of her being), she cannot assimilate experience. Compliancy thus becomes for Evelina a deviant form of prudence that violates any practical wisdom.[7]

Knowing nothing of the world suggests a state of unreflective union with nature prior to knowledge. This state of unselfconsciousness contrasts with a succeeding stage of irretrievable loss in which the emergent self stands over against the world. Indeed, to act only from the "impulses of Nature" accords with those older patriarchal notions of the feminine as well as our common sense precept of innocence ("Nature in her simplest attire"). Within such a limited, cultural stereotype for female behavior Evelina authors her journal-diary and retrieves in the act of writing a richness of experience otherwise denied to her. In the gap between her speech and action, between her disclaimers of experience and her writing of a journal-diary, one can hear a frustrated desire that seeks to be recognized: what will emerge as both problem and promise is Evelina's namelessness as a metonym for her absence from patriarchal language.

Through the social void opened up by that gap, Evelina discovers that both she and her history can be (re)figured by her own act of writing. For that reason, writing an account of her experiences shatters the rigid concept of woman that she begins with. Writing her journal-letters will liberate Evelina from the alienating self-consciousness that divides her from herself; it will release her to the company of the two-in-one of thought—a process denied the rest of Burney's represented heroines.

What needs to be carefully traced before one can understand the significance of Evelina's journal is how, at first, she relinquishes experience for the sake of concealing herself in innocence. In her early forays into the world, the assailed heroine's intentional focus upon artlessness obscures the transparency of the natural self that she wishes to project. In effect, to act only from "the impulses of Nature" is to perform, as well as to invite, oppression.[8] Furthermore, any binary economy of female innocence–male oppression overlooks Evelina's calculated innocence and concealed experience. Only at a point of crisis near to hysteria, when she is forced to write on her own behalf, does Evelina begin to understand how concealment does not prevent her from revealing herself—to herself, as well as to others. Even as Evelina narrates a representational myth in which the one narrated is caught in the female self-identity/male repression dichotomy, as writer she questions the essentialism underlying that binary economy.

The novel opens with the cultural definition that outlines Evelina's intrinsically innocent character. Reverend Villars describes his adopted ward, setting forth in little the problem of the female in eighteenth-century society: "This artless young creature, with too much beauty to escape notice, has too much sensibility to be indifferent to it; but she has too little wealth to be sought with propriety by men of the fashionable world" (8). He explains the "peculiar cruelty of her situation" as "only child of a wealthy Baronet, whose person she has never seen, whose character she has reason to abhor, and whose name she is forbidden to claim; entitled as she is to lawfully inherit his fortune and estate, is there any probability that he will *properly* own her?" Artlessness and beauty without wealth and name is not only Evelina's global condition; it is also the charm of her appeal, the only marketable asset she has, and the greatest danger to her character.

Evelina's social position teeters precariously between legitimacy and bastardy; although she is the legitimate daughter of a baronet, her mother's legal marriage remains unacknowledged by her father. Adopted by a country parson, she can't claim social rank with such modest means. Her namelessness—a form of social silence—creates the conflict in the novel. More than a social deficiency, namelessness functions symbolically for the patriarchy that constitutes the "named." As a metonym for woman, it stands in the way of Evelina's social acceptance and inhibits her ability to name herself other than within the category of innocence, the character given to her by her culture.

The question of character and its rival conceptions immediately emerge. Is Evelina to be described as a traditional fictional entity created and controlled by an author—even an author in the form of a dominant culture who authors her? Is she an autonomous person, a "real identity," who speaks and acts by her own authority? Is she a purely linguistic construction?[9] Each of these notions of character fails to describe adequately the generative power of naming that multiplies the company of Evelina within the free play of writing.[10]

Preserving Evelina's singularly innocent name seems mandated by all those in the novel concerned with the continuity of the social order. For example, Villars's wish to have Evelina returned from her social experiences unchanged, still "all innocence" (110), implies sacrificing the seasoning of practical knowledge on the patriarchal altar of pristine ignorance. All he asks from Lady Howard in sending her his Evelina as "innocent as angel, and artless as purity itself," is that she will return his child "as you receive her." Lady Howard reassuringly agrees with Villars that Evelina is indeed "truly ingenuous and simple" with "a certain air of inexperience and innocency" (10). Launched into the world, Evelina should somehow expand her experience, but without the loss of her intrinsic, encapsulated innocence. "The world," says Villars to Evelina, "is the general harbour of fraud and of folly, of duplicity and of impertinence" where "the artlessness of your nature, and the simplicity of your education alike *unfit* you for its thorny path" (104, 105; emphasis added). A properly feminine, bourgeois "education" assures one of a perspective "unfit" for the intrigues of society. Villars holds an unshakable belief in Evelina's essentialistic innocence and hopes that she may be an "ornament" of delight to family, friends, and neighbors, "employing herself in useful and innocent occupations" (105). Above all else, he cautions her to retain her "genuine simplicity." But we will see by Evelina's own account of her first social forays that she is not as devoid of practical wisdom or as unfit for society as she, and everyone else, assumes.

In writing about her first ball to Villars, Evelina finds male behavior so "provoking" that she determines not to dance at all rather than seem to be "humouring" male condescension (18). Her reaction is more than the shock of innocence at the disportment of behavior outside the bounds of her experience, for she interprets what she sees as an assumption of superiority toward women. Rather than lacking awareness about the situation at hand, she is lacking information about social propriety. The fact that her account to Villars focuses not on ignorance of social sanctions but on her interpretation of human incivility proves this point.[11] In this respect, her response is spontaneous but not discriminating, intuitively just, but not socially correct.

Evelina's reflexive ability to read more than one possible meaning in otherwise socially correct behavior refutes any Lockean notion that innocence is a tabula rasa upon which an accumulating experience is engraved. Although Evelina recognizes hypocrisy (Mr. Lovel), bad taste (the Branghtons), male impertinence (Willoughby), and female constraints (codes of propriety), time and again she retreats into the blankness of self-conscious confusion, silence, and the unformed feature of innocence, as when she meets Lord Orville:

How will he be provoked, thought I, when he finds what a simple rustic he has honoured with his choice! one whose ignorance of the world makes her perpetually fear doing something wrong! (19)

But while castigating her own behavior, Evelina exhibits an assimilative, interpretive grasp, as when the thought occurs to her that Orville did choose her, "insignificant as I was, compared to a man of his rank and figure." This ready adaptability to fit herself to new social situations is belied by the way her letters attire her in an innocence bordering on the hysterical. Furthermore, that correct social appearance includes a contradictory comportment of innocence: unworldy enough to appear guileless or diffident, yet sophisticated enough to recognize dissimulation and artifice; subtle

enough to discern deception and fraud, and poised enough to with-
stand male aggression.

From Evelina's writing about her very first ball, we can see that
though ignorant of social decorum, she is not devoid of perception.
We are led to think otherwise when Villars's letters array her in
artlessness. Whenever Evelina is abashed with shyness or outraged
at male impropriety toward her person, she does the same. On such
occasions, she cloaks her feelings in the more artless raiment of
silence even as she discloses them in her writing: "But I was silent,
for I knew not what I ought to say" (141). As she enters an already
established symbolic order and submits her desire to the pressures
of that order, adopting a conventional conceptual wardrobe, fur-
nishing herself with a language that has already determined who
she is, she allows her reflections to be covered over by the veneer
of naïveté.

This acquiescence, a very imprudent prudence, precipitates her
disasters. Lord Orville's attentions, in part an attempt to test her
capability to speak, merely create a restraint that causes her to lapse
into silence. Ignorant of the impropriety entailed in refusing one
dance partner and accepting another, Evelina generates male judgments ranging from "beautiful" to "ill-bred," "intelligent" to "rustic," or in Orville's case, from "ignorant or mischievous" to "a poor
weak girl" (24, 25). To submit to the pressure for female silence
contributes to her appearance of artlessness, a commodity valuable
to the patriarchal appetite for the natural, as, for example, when
Orville later says of Evelina that "she is too young for suspicion,
and has an artlessness of disposition I never saw equalled" (328).
She discovers early, however, that an uncalculated artlessness is un-
readable by others without the accompanying signs of reflection in
her that would prevent misreading *artless* for *artifice*. Smarting from
the effects of her own innocent guise, Evelina writes that she wishes
to flee London, convincing herself that she now finds it "tiresome."

If Evelina's inexperience causes her embarrassment and real anguish, so does pretending to an experience that would conceal her
genuine lack of worldly tempering. This posturing reveals itself when
she attempts to elude the impertinent attentions of the lecherous Sir
Clement Willoughby. She imitates fashionable manners, but her
artifice cannot match Willoughby's rakishness. Here is a much keener
male adversary than any she has met before, and one who epitomizes

the fraud and duplicity Villars worries about. Her "peevish" indignation only charms the rake into further importunities toward one whose "airs" heighten her beauty. Merely exchanging innocence for sophistication does not solve the problem of being turned—or turning oneself—into an object for exploitation.

Evelina concludes her London letters to Villars with the plaint: "I am too inexperienced and ignorant to conduct myself with propriety in this town, where everything is new to me, and many things are unaccountable and perplexing" (37). Though her comment testifies to the inadequacy of *any* concept of female innocence that excludes an experiential understanding, it also clearly demonstrates a view that oscillates between the perspectives of innocence and experience. Claiming confusion admits to an articulated need for understanding experience—and therefore admits to how much she already understands it.[12]

Even when displeased with her narrated ignorance, Villars is quite aware of Evelina's narrative understanding; her persuasive writing is enough to convince him of her budding wisdom. Nevertheless, he answers her letter with a postscripted prayer that artlessness or "gaiety of heart" will remain hers (44). It is not only Evelina who feels compelled to overwrite her experience with the inscription of innocence—it is Villars's religious and moral clothing as well.

The contrast between Evelina's practical wisdom and others' dullness sharpens when she meets her wealthy but vulgar grandmother and her middle-class shopkeeping relatives. The Branghtons display all the ignorant excesses of grasping bourgeois social climbers without any of the intelligence that could redeem them. Their vulgarity and lack of manners vividly contrast Evelina's grace, refinement, modesty, and quickness. Willfully ignorant of decorum governing opera, they embarrass Evelina with their stingy selection of seats, lack of civility and proper attire. Offensive at every turn, they even arouse our sympathy for her when she rushes into Willoughby's arms to escape them. At the same time, however, the Branghtons' doggedly unrefined appetites attest to Evelina's fuller understanding of those social nuances that remain unarticulated. Indeed, such outrageous, low, and vulgar behavior spontaneously prompts her will, passion, and tongue: "This family is so low-bred and vulgar, that I should be equally ashamed of such a connection in the country, or anywhere" (83).

When straining to recommend herself to males, however, Evelina postures in the language and comportment of the idealized female for whom discrimination is forbidden. She fails to distinguish between acquiring the accoutrements of innocence and *being* innocent, a standard that forces her into an anxious mode and wears away her spontaneity. Even though Evelina can understand a bold stare, even from a mighty lord, to be a "look of libertinism toward women" (102), she seems almost willfully to overlook sexual dangers. Her awareness, significantly, does not extend to the sexual-social threat in accepting, although under some duress, Willoughby's offer to drive her home unescorted or in accompanying the Branghton girls into the darkened alleys of Vauxhall. This gap in her understanding points to the broader issue of how the conceptual model of vulnerable innocence conceals from a female not only her own sexual desire but her sexual power as well. The patriarchal model for female virtue appears to posit innocence merely in order to assault it, so that lecherous Willoughby can silence Evelina's objections by invoking the patriarchal code designed to protect her (85). Thus, when Orville discovers her alone with the rake, she "was not at liberty to assign any reason" for her ambiguous behavior (89). An unarticulated injunction against understanding, as well as interpreting, herself to others lies at the core of her repressed desperation and anguish. Merely deferring to male authority encourages misinterpretation, accedes to an unconscious presumption of her own innocence, and attests to the ambiguity inherent in consciously maintaining a vicious form of female virtue: permanent naïveté.

We learn then, very early in the novel that Evelina is persuasively observant, often aware of the role she plays in creating equivocal situations. Evelina and those representing her culture have mutually, though not always overtly, collaborated to grant her a character that denies the richness of archetype by confining it to stereotype. Above all else, reflective thought must be excluded from a conception of female virtue.[13] It is no surprise then that attending Congreve's *Love for Love* puts her out of countenance, paralyzes her with silence, prevents her from observing. This is not a play, Orville says, that "can be honoured with their [the ladies'] approbation"; the young ladies in question must keep their observations to themselves in order to keep their innocence intact (69). Despite Orville's injunction against honoring the risqué play with female approbation, Evelina *writes* that it was "fraught with wit and entertainment" (67). She also admits to Villars in another letter how her own virtue "must seem rather to invite than to forbid the offers and notice I received; and yet, so great was my apprehension of this interpretation, that I am sure, my dear Sir, you would have laughed had you seen how proudly grave I appeared" (208).

In spite of such astute reasoning, in every situation where Lord Orville sees but does not hear her, her represented (cultivated) artlessness veils her in an ambiguous silence that invites attack. Overlooking the obvious sexual threat, Evelina reluctantly agrees to accompany the vulgar Branghton girls into the darkened alleys of Vauxhall. Accosted by a group of rowdy wags bent upon the plunder of innocence, Evelina once again flies off with Willoughby into an even darker alley. Although outraged at his predatory impertinence, at the implied sexual innuendo that seeks to cut off her response, she cannot refute the stinging correctness of his satire: "Is this a place for Miss Anville?—these dark walks!—no party! no companions!" Mr. Branghton puts it more bluntly: "You must all of you have had a mind to be affronted" (185). "A mind to be affronted" rationalizes its complicity by taking refuge in the role of female victim. We can be outraged at Willoughby's verbal power play, but we cannot discount the truth of what he says. Willoughby himself testifies to Evelina's wisdom: "Let Miss Anville look to herself; she has an excellent understanding, and needs no counselor" (328). But the weight of social codes and conceptual models is too much for someone who must adhere to a narrow female standard.[14]

Whenever Evelina relinquishes the authority of her own experience in favor of a naive sexual facade, she draws from others an opposing aggressiveness. After a fireworks display at Marybone Gardens, Evelina once again rushes off in a fright, heedless of remaining with her companions. Various "bold and unfeeling" men accost her, and she runs hastily to some questionable women for refuge. It is revealing that she protests her inability to free herself from their strong grip, and yet as soon as she is recognized by Orville, she finds the strength to tear herself away. With consternation and a measure of disingenuousness she later writes, "How strangely, how cruelly have all appearances turned against me! Had I been blessed with any presence of mind, I should instantly have explained to him the accident which occasioned my being in such terrible company:—

but I have none!" (222). If courage has deserted her in this incident, so has the memory of similar experiences. To Villars, she deplores her lack of "presence of mind" (222), while forgetting that "presence of mind" responds spontaneously to the situation at hand, but persistently believing what she ought to be supersedes what she needs to do. If further proof that Evelina has guessed full well what kind of "ladies" she has been with is needed, she provides it when amused at Madame Duval's ignorance of them: "Indeed, it is wonderful to see how easily and how frequently she is deceived" (221).

Doomed to fly from one dangerous and improper situation into another, Evelina seems inflexibly passive in her resignation to "properly own" the female name she has adopted, in spite of growing experiental evidence that this name does not serve her best interests any more than her namelessness does.[15] If Evelina needs to learn to overcome a passive role, she also needs to acknowledge that passivity and innocence are anything but powerless. Mrs. Selwyn, a delightfully satirical version of woman, comments that Evelina's appearance seems coquettish and creates confusion: "You, innocent as you pretend to look, are the cause" (310). When Evelina departs from Clifton in order to flee Orville, the same event viewed from Mrs. Selwyn's perspective is seen as "the logic of coquetry" crafted to captivate Orville (360). Seeing herself as a victim only, that is, as an unaccountable participant, however involuntary that participation may be, reduces the richer possibilities for action that would fit Evelina *for* the world and not just *to* it. In the social arena where she must display herself as a nameless (valueless) commodity until she can acquire nameability, however, she is often overwhelmed by the harshness of a world based upon a conceptual model that categorizes her by gender, calculates her visible worth, names her as nameless, and thereby condemns her to a passive silence by speaking for her.

The Evelina so named (represented) in the journal, however, is not the one who intrigues us as much as the who that narrates and orders the events by writing about them. The Evelina who writes reveals a much more evaluative knowledge of her world than the Evelina she writes about. As the account of Mrs. Stanley's ball has shown, Evelina is not without judgment, wit, and quick intelligence. As her accounts of the Branghtons show, she is brighter, more sensitive, and perceptive than they could ever hope to be. Her journal reveals that the most intelligent men, Orville and Willoughby, do appreciate her understanding in spite of her inexperience. Furthermore, when describing the witty Mrs. Selwyn's satirical forays, the Evelina who writes is more discriminating than the older lady who seems unaware of the censure her bent for irony invites. The ability to converse by writing to "two in good company," the oneself who asks and the oneself who answers, by traveling back and forth through the gap created by speech and writing, enables Evelina to find a path through the horrific void that namelessness implies.

A central episode involving the use and authority of Evelina's name marks a turn in her understanding of herself, a turn away from any self constructed as a singular entity, and also marks the intersection between the Evelina narrated and the who that narrates. The Branghtons learn of her acquaintance with Lord Orville and insist upon taking advantage of that relationship in order to usurp the social meaning of her name when they call on Lord Orville to solicit his business for the family shop. She writes to Villars: "I could have met with no accident that would so cruelly have tormented me" (232). This threat is even more serious than the sexual dangers she has encountered. Until now, Evelina's own essentialistic awareness of herself as an innocent has prevented her from fully recognizing the self-objectification enforced by that definition. The overt reification of her as a "device" available to the utility and consumption of bourgeois economy, another form of namelessness, presses upon her what she would otherwise wish to conceal from herself.[16] She cries out: "By what authority did you take such a liberty," and, "who gave you leave?—who desired you?" (233). At this instance the subdued and repressed hysteria percolating at the edges of the narrative boils to the surface. For perhaps the first time in the novel, Evelina claims her own right to the disclosing as well as the concealing power of name and discourse. To speak importunately to Orville "as comes from one Miss Anville" (233), makes her name an item in the Branghton trade. It forces her to act to lay aside the disguise of female passivity.

Usurping and reifying Evelina's name graphically illustrates how a narrowly defined, passive female role but poorly serves her, causing her to forfeit Orville's good opinion and giving him "reason to suppose I presumed to boast of his acquaintance!" "Half frantic," driven "wild," suffering an "irreparable injury" (234), Evelina eschews the codes of both female decorum and virtue and writes to

Orville directly. Forced to assert herself to prevent an inauthentic mode of discourse, namely reification, she nonetheless is impeded when her status as a nameless female undercuts her authority to name, that is, to articulate and interpret herself to others. To the Branghtons she may insist, "I must take the liberty to request, that my name may never be made use of without my knowledge," but in experience her name as female consists of those qualities and traits attributed *to* her rather than *by* her (236). Evelina closes her letter to Orville with a plaintive acknowledgment that she was used as the "instrument, however innocently, of so much trouble." When the letter is purloined by Willoughby just as her name was usurped by the Branghtons, it erupts from the silence relegated to a female, domestic circle of family and friends and into the din of a male, public circulation. The letter and its erratic and unforeseen postings radically alter the message Evelina has been sending about herself— to others as well as herself.[17]

II

This central episode introduces the purloined letter and the forged reply. The letter never reaches Orville because Willoughby purloins it, forges an impertinent answer, and signs Orville's name. Woman's letter, her "name" is purloined through Willoughby by the patriarchal "name of the father."[18]

When Evelina's letter is diverted from its path, it becomes purloined in another sense. *Pur-loigner* in the French means to put aside or put amiss, to suffer, a letter in sufferance trapped in a discourse it does not initiate, a letter effectively silenced. So trapped, Evelina herself becomes a letter in sufferance.[19] Nonetheless, when the letter is diverted from its "proper" course, it does not cease to function. Evelina's letter overreaches authorial intention and male possession, initiating a chain of unpredictable changes in whoever comes to read it. She intends her letter to represent her "truely" to Orville, whereas Willoughby intends his letter persuasively to present Orville as different from the man himself. In each case, the one who comes to possess the letter is determined by it. Although the forged reply at first delights Evelina, Evelina's letter comes to possess Willoughby. In holding her letter, Willoughby hides her and her possibilities and becomes possessed by what he possesses without authority. In holding the false letter, Evelina comes to a clearer understanding of the real Orville. The letter stirs desire and, in some sense, rewrites all their lives. Even at the end of the novel, Evelina's letter still has the power to cost someone's life in a duel.

At first perusal, as Evelina ruefully admits, the forged reply delights her. She marks only its expressions of regard because they answer to her own desires:

> It gave me no sensation but of delight. . . . I only marked the expressions of his own regard . . . repeating to myself, 'Good God, is it possible?—am I then loved by Lord Orville?' (242)

In a second reading, "every word changed,—it did not seem the same letter." She recalls, furthermore, the circumstances surrounding the receipt of the letter:

> Had this letter been the most respectful that could be written, the clandestine air given to it, by his proposal of sending his servant for my answer, instead of having it directed to his house, would effectually have prevented my writing. (245)

In the forgery, Willoughby speaks for Orville, in his name, to discredit his authority and to conceal Evelina's "capacity": "I concealed your letter to prevent a discovery of your capacity; and I wrote you an answer, which I hoped would prevent your wishing for any other" (370). It bears a "clandestine air" because it tries to divert her response, to prevent her from "having it directed to [Orville's] house." Once again the forged letter conceals Evelina, requiring her to envelop herself in innocence, to post herself into danger. In purloining her letter he silences her, denies her voice and name.

Nevertheless, words are changed by changing contexts, and when she and Orville meet in Bristol, Evelina rejects the forgery, rejects Villars's abstractions about character, and lets observation guide her judgment. Accordingly, she can interpret the letter more accurately in writing about it. Evelina recognizes in this concrete event how innocence can be a "false delicacy which occasioned my silence." Writing opens to her a horizon of experience beyond the literal reading of the text, beyond the sense corresponding to her desire, beyond the sense of the "Orville" presented to her. Although the words in the forged letter remain unchanged, the meaning of them does not. When she rethinks the situation by writing about it, Villars's reply and Orville's past actions change the significance of the false letter.

When Evelina meets Orville face to face, her proper, intended coldness and reserve melt away and she writes Villars:

> It was my intention, nay, my endeavour, to support them with firmness: but when I formed the plan, I thought only of the letter,—not of Lord Orville. (264)

In rejecting the false letter as a misrepresentation of Orville, Evelina acts from the stronger conviction that she knows him through a broader context of experience—character, regard, comportment.

The meaning, then, of the letter resides in the relations among sender, receiver, and holder, a communal bond that enmeshes in its web whoever comes in contact with it. When Willoughby purloins Evelina's letter, he is only the most outrageous (and hence useful) instance of a social order that in speaking for her, in owning the signs that signify her, in using namelessness as a sign of woman as currency, purloins her letter. In *The Rape of Clarissa,* Terry Eagleton conjoins writing and woman:

> The problem of writing is in this sense the problem of the woman: how is she to be at once decorous and spontaneous, translucently candid yet subdued to social pressure? Writing, like women, marks a frontier between public and private, at once agonized outpouring and prudent stratagem. (46)

Through the dialogic agency of a letter as both "agonized outpouring and prudent stratagem" and of her own journal, "decorous and spontaneous, translucently candid yet subdued to social pressure," Evelina better understands the consequences of her misrepresentation. Moreover, she recognizes that silence transforms her into a victim and exacerbates her sufferings; silence does not prevent her self-revelation when she admits that behavior, mood, and other nonverbal gestures create a horizon of possible meaning for Orville to interpret: "I tremble lest he should misconstrue my reserve for embarrassment!" (259). And again, "I could not endure he should make his own interpretation of my silence" (281).

Writing gives Evelina an opportunity to speak, lending her a voice that the world not only denies but insists she doesn't have. She does not simply record what confounds her in London—a form of spectatorship—she participates in reordering what puzzles and frightens her. In writing, Evelina learns that she is capable of thought and therefore capable of speech, and she says this in the very process of denying it: "I will talk,—write,—think of him no more!" (247). These disclaimers cause Villars to miss the strength and achievement of Evelina's letters. He unwittingly acknowledges their authority by simply accepting them as representational, as veridical accounts. The persuasive power of her narration compensates for the authority that silences her. She corresponds because her experiences do not— *discordia concors.*

At times the dazzling power of narration causes Evelina to fall back upon that reductive concept of female innocence, laying claim to the unambiguous and literal, draping herself in self-illusion. To discover that writing uncovers what has been carefully concealed from oneself can be very disconcerting: "I will not write any longer; for the more I think ... the less indifferent ... I find myself" (13). Writing begins to find for her, her self. What she cannot see, perhaps what at times she *will* not see is that transparency and innocence are available only within experience. The greater her vocabulary of experience, the broader her perspective on a situation, the more she understands the power and attendant dangers of innocence. Writing enables Evelina to share in the composition of her own destiny, to see that the role of innocent bystander is often complicitous with that of active participant.

Writing as act precludes her being a passive spectator: she is enmeshed in a web of discourse that calls for her response, that connects her to her particular place in culture. Writing reliably guides or opens her to possible modes of female conduct. When Villars warns Evelina against "those regions of fancy and passion whither her new guide conducted her," he also implies that writing informs experience, since her new "guide" is her imaginative pen— not patriarchal advice. Since the letters themselves not only reside in but *are* the "regions of fancy and passion," they are not as easily subject to the discursive control of patriarchal logic. Neither are they

limited to the linear movement of a conventional plot, a sending
that asks for no reply. In fact, the episodic zigzag movement of
epistolary narrative resists any overarching structure targeted as plot.
The epistolary shapes pathos, terror, emotion in such a way as to
discourage the reader from building theoretical constructions of analysis upon it. Her letters are not a form for imperatives, statements
of facts, or assertions. The indirection of the culturally unsayable
opens "regions of fancy and passion."

Feelings are less a subject Evelina takes *up* than an affective
condition that takes *her*. "I made a resolution, when I began, that
I would not be urgent; but my pen—or rather my thoughts, will
not suffer me to keep it—" (13). Writing does not merely record her
feelings for Orville, it shapes them, gives space for the feelings that
draw her into dark alleys. Writing reveals to her—and others—the
pattern of her desires. Villars, Maria, and we are sure she is in
love, even though she has never admitted to it openly: "Long . . .
have I perceived the ascendancy which Lord Orville has gained upon
your mind" (290). Evelina writes to Villars but finds herself addressing Orville:

> Oh! Lord Orville!—it shall be the sole study of my happy life,
> to express, better than by words, the sense I have of your exalted
> benevolence and greatness of mind! (369)

As Evelina's writing becomes a displacement for her concealed desires, it opens her to more than one identity, more than one version
of character. It draws her out of the stifling closet of female reserve
and into multiple chambers of thought.

The company of thought is available to Evelina through the conversation of her writing. This conversation enables Evelina to discover a counter-authority to that of the patriarchy. Usually when
Evelina's discourse falls silent due to lack of authority, it is Villars,
much like Burney's father, who feels authorized to speak for her. His
letters to Evelina are filled with maxims, exhortations, and the highest sentiments of concern and moral propriety. Ever admonishing,
he simply cannot forbear talking about "the right line of conduct,"
the same for both sexes, "though the manner in which it is pursued
may somewhat vary." The varied "manner" in which "the right line
of conduct" is pursued not only attests to the inadequacy of any

"right line of conduct" as a guide for females but also to the impossibility of only one "right line." Nonetheless, even Villars is persuaded by Evelina's narrative power so that, when she writes about male importunity, he admonishes her to take authority in the sense of responsibility to her own experience to learn from it:

> But you must learn not only to *judge* but to *act* for yourself; if any schemes are started, any engagements made, which your understanding represents to you as improper, *exert* yourself resolutely in avoiding them; and do not, by a *too passive* facility, risk the censure of the world, or your own future regret. (149; emphasis added)

In an astonishing admission, Villars explains to Evelina that innocence *conceals* the approach of duplicity: "Guileless yourself, how could you prepare against the duplicity of another? Your disappointment has but been proportioned . . . to the innocence which hid its approach" (253). He repines: "That innocence . . . should, of all others, be the blindest to its own danger,—the most exposed to treachery,—and the least able to defend itself, in a world where it is little known, less valued, and perpetually deceived!" (289). Innocence, he implies, nurtures hysteria. Evelina's persuasive narration holds an authority that forces Villars to redefine his cherished concept of female innocence.

The dialogue generated by these letters shows how writing addresses an important issue far beyond the need to express or the purpose of guidance—especially since Evelina often does not respond in her letters to the advice he gives. Her realistic descriptions and astute assessments of human behavior convince Villars of the authority of her writing even as he tries to maintain the fiction of her artlessness. He consistently displaces Evelina's authority, standing *in* for her but not letting her stand *up* for herself. Renouncing such a patriarchal version of authority can be the means for woman to name herself rather than let others name her.

Although Villars may speak for Evelina when she cannot, *speaking for* is not the same as *letting* speak. Evelina's letters are authoritative precisely to the extent to which they are filled with concrete, but ever-changing, interpretations of particular events.[20] When pressed by Evelina's details concerning actual events, Villars is forced to relinquish his abstractions for more practical considerations that are

attuned to the present need. Her authority corresponds to the way
her letters say what *is* rather than what ought to be. Evelina's letter
about Willoughby is so persuasive that it even moves Villars to
relinquish the patriarchal mandate for female reserve:

> It is not sufficient for you to be reserved: his conduct even calls
> for your resentment; and should he again, as will doubtless be
> his endeavour, contrive to solicit your favour in private, let your
> disdain and displeasure be so marked, as to constrain a change
> in his behaviour. (147)

In other words, female virtue encompasses more than a silent reserve;
virtue takes the active form of a disdain and displeasure so marked
that it will force a behavioral change in others. Concealing the
strength of a woman's own desires and intelligence diminishes her
human richness; she remains one-dimensional as long as she is complicitous with the representational model.

In writing, Evelina finds the connections, the parallels, and the
patterns of events that shape her experience to herself and her co-
respondents. In writing, Evelina can explain and defend how she
behaved at her first ball, although she could never do so by speaking
directly to those who received a wrong impression of her. In a letter
she can discuss her disapprobation of people, places, and events,
expressing attitudes and opinions that she must otherwise hide or
dissemble. The letter privately gratifies, frees her discourse from
what must otherwise adhere to social strictures. Eagleton states that
a decorum of who may write to whom, and under what conditions,
provides an internal censorship, since the epistle is at heart an appeal
to another (46). Since Evelina writes the bulk of her letters to Villars
who represents the authority of patriarchy, she allows the dialogue
to speak for her rather than give him the impression she is making
judgments. By seeming to record whole conversations, she lets the
rhetoric of the letter ameliorate the impertinence of its own intimate
revelation.[21] Her epistles subversively charm more than her strained
efforts to be artless; the more her letters express a deeply felt private
sentiment, the more they snare the reader into a reciprocal intimacy.

Evelina allows the dialogue to speak indirectly for her rather than
playing author in the patriarchal sense.[22] She criticizes the authorial
model, nonetheless, when she, like Burney, deliberately conceals her

authority by editing or merely recording events in the form of private letters. Evelina's (non)authority becomes a viable alternative not only to the power exercised by males, but to that of the other women as well. Madame Duval's access to society rests entirely upon her patrilineal name and money, for which she is more tolerated than accepted. Lady Howard can speak with the authority of the patrilineal name, money, and position. She therefore does not test the limits of masculine authority. Though Mrs. Selwyn thrives on satirical challenges to authority, she is indulged for the sake of name and position. These versions of female power rely on an idea of identity coextensive with patriarchy. The forced race of the nameless old women servants, so often puzzling to readers, demonstrates the plight of woman without resource to male legitimation. The argument here is that Evelina, by contrast, opens up a non-patriarchal path for identity and authority through the company of the letter's conversation.

The novel is about sendings, letters; hence a novel without author(ity), only an editor.[23] In both Burney's preface and Evelina's narrative, authority is renounced. What is true of the letters is true of the novel: neither Evelina, the one narrated and the one narrating, nor Burney authors it in the sense of origin and closure. They send letters—one sends to Berry Hill, one into the world—but they do not speak for others. They let others speak for themselves and keep the conversation going. They listen to the world and send letters as a function of listening. Evelina narrates: in letting the others speak she must listen and understand them better perhaps than they understand themselves. She makes Mrs. Selwyn's irony her own, makes Branghton vulgarity part of her world even as she dismisses it; she even assimilates the aggression of the male and the displacement of woman to this narrated world. She is author in the ancient sense of *auctor,* one who augments the conversation underway, one who need not command or coerce to make herself heard.

With the help of her new guide, Evelina discovers how she can resist any "plot" ready formed for her. It enables her to say who she is in spite of cultural limits upon her discourse. The intimacy of the letter creates the impression of saying what was not intended to be heard, what she is not authorized to say. Thus, she can use writing as a form of cultural power to disarm cherished notions rather than wresting them from the grip of the opposition. The patriarchal authorities, those "magistrates of the press, and Censors for the public" (original preface), merely assert what ought to be, while Evelina describes what is, that is, what appears. This opening for what appears, for further dialogue, prevents any determinant meaning. The Evelina narrated and the one who narrates, Villars, Maria, Burney, and imagination, the new guide, all symbolize the intersubjective relations that expropriate the individual.

Narrating names who she is long before her father or her husband give her an authorized, patrilineal name. But the narrative is not public, else it couldn't be written—or is public only by editorial intervention. Like Evelina's unauthorized being, her letters are unauthorized, private appeals to another, protected by an internal censorship:

> I gave over the attempt of reading . . . and, having no voice to answer the enquiries of Lord Orville, I put the letter into his hands, and *left it to speak both for me and itself.* (386; emphasis added)

Otherwise they would be indecorous, even impertinent. Thus the narrating Evelina outgrows the already narrated innocent angel whom others wish to preserve.

Burney may purloin Evelina's letters by editing them, and we may eavesdrop. Like Willoughby, we may be claimed, drawn into the narrative conversation by overhearing her, but she does not intend the world to hear what she is not authorized to say. Instead, Evelina's authority is revealed as that of character in the ancient sense of ethos. It is based upon everything we as readers know about her: her represented and representing self, her shrewdness in oscillating between those two selves. Ethos emerges as a provisional identity, in between the narrator/narrated, in between author/editor Burney, between the different sendings. Burney's narrative about Evelina writing a narrative about herself is not properly named or fathered;[24] like that of Evelina, it is "unnamed, unknown without any sort of recommendation" (original preface), an "other" message. Evelina's letter was purloined at birth, and her search is for a legitimate name, a voice that is authentically her own.

Evelina cannot authenticate her own narrative according to the patriarchal standards for authority and legitimacy.[25] To do so would open her to dangers which patrilineal name, position, and money

would otherwise circumvent. It would also open her to the censure
that Mrs. Selwyn's irony receives. Jean-François Lyotard helps us
say what is at stake in this narrative at a high level of generality,
and hence, at a broad level of applicability. Legitimation, he observes, is the process of deciding the true and the false.[26] Representation and its rational criterion of adequacy or accuracy is
masculine—an Enlightenment ideal. In the Enlightenment culture
of Burney's age, narrative knowledge lacks legitimacy and belongs
to "fables, myths, legends, fit only for women and children"
(Lyotard, 27). However, narrative knowledge lies behind, is presup-
posed by, such rational discourse. It reveals the significant shape of
human life in that all questions of truth are situated in events that
have enough coherence to be told as a narrative. The events and
their connections are not veridical; rather they are events of vision,
the a priori context for representational discourse.

It is no accident that women who, like Evelina, cannot control
signification write letters that forestall closure and keep the conversation in good company. As Evelina's letters displace her as a constituted entity, they become communally constitutive. Each sending
replaces the previous one so that ideological structures cannot censor
them. Thus they mediate all conceptual boundaries—public, private,
self, world.[27] Instead of embalming the world in patriarchy's sterile
discourse, the name of the father, these generative women—Evelina,
Caroline Evelyn, Fanny Burney—give it birth, even beyond their
own mortality.

Women's purloinable letter, like an unnamed child without a legitimating birthright, reveals there is no fixed identity at either end
of the co-respondence. Evelina's birthright cannot be subject to such
a public or legal claim, for if it were, it would violate the rule of
female propriety, damage her father's honor, and call her own legitimacy into question. She must rely, instead, on private intercession
by others who speak on her behalf. Yet, what convinces Sir John
Belmont that Evelina is his daughter is not Mrs. Selwyn's argument,
not a legal claim, not even an appeal to pathos. It is Evelina's
resemblance to her mother, a truth that destroys his narrative by
substituting another—by refiguring his life. That is, her most convincing proof is neither a document nor a form of patriarchal speech
that bears the silencing authority of a truth statement. She posts a
likeness of her mother that lacks any of those patrilineal seals of

legitimation. Caroline Evelyn's letter, read by John Belmont years after her death, is shattering: "Ten thousand daggers could not have wounded me like this letter" (367). Evelina's legitimacy rests on a revolutionary displacement of the criterion of legitimacy inherent in patriarchal culture. It rests upon her own renunciation of the patriarchal authority that diminishes rather than augments when it insists upon power over discourse. Though she seems to sink into the conventional patrilineal family and ends her story, "I have time for no more [writing]" (388), her lack of name and of the means by which her name is recovered opens a countercultural possibility for narrating ourselves without the authoritative subject at either end of the writing and conversing process. The representative heroine is subverted by her own act of representing.

We have seen that any notion of the female as a singular, stable entity is radically altered by Evelina's writing. In writing, the representational Evelina is exposed as a reductive concept, a product of the narrowly mediated, patriarchal code. Uncritically assuming that the individual is fully present as given, that representation is the ontological determination of woman, ensures an utterly predictable crisis for, and plot against, women. That plot, woman's silence, her repressed hysteria, hides possible self-discovery when it makes her nameable, sayable only by the linguistically mediated form available to her. As long as woman lacks a voice in the sense of sharing in the cultural figuration of who she is, she can never be an active conveyor of meaning. Indirection by means of writing without closure allows the forbidden unsayable to be said. Julia Kristeva writes: "In 'woman' I see something that cannot be represented, something that is not said, something above and beyond nomenclature and ideologies."[28] Yet, every time "nomenclature and ideologies" fail women, they speak indirectly of woman's inexhaustibility and subvert their own representation of woman. Revealed and concealed in any concept of woman is the open possibility for an ongoing, ever incomplete and incompletable identity. That possibility lies in writing, for, more than marks upon a page, writing calls forth the generative power of name—all that woman is and can be and is not yet; all about her that has been overlooked and yet is to be said.

In the next two chapters, we will see how female silence is breached by a sensibility that not only resists the rational but challenges it as well. Examination of key episodes in *Camilla* and *Cecilia* shows that the two female characters, in anguish because of their inability to speak or to name according to the conceptual model of representation, must resort to indirect means, gaps in the public discourse, fits of madness, sickness near to death, and exhibitions of emotion in order to be heard and understood. The fissures created in these novels bring the nonrational near, establish affective communal bonds, and allow an opening for the female voice of suffering, of mood, and of sensibility which has effectively been silenced.

2

Cecilia: *The Madness of Reason*

Why wilt thou Examine every little fibre of my soul
Spreading them out before the Sun like Stalks of flax to
*   dry*
Thou wilt go mad with horror if thou dost Examine thus
                    —William Blake, "The Four Zoas"

THE CRISIS IN *Cecilia* stems from the terms of a will that makes her
an heiress "with no other restriction than that of annexing her name,
if she married, to the disposal of her hand and her riches."[1] At the
time the book was published in 1782, the question widely debated
was whether or not the change from the noble name of Delvile to
the genteel name of Beverley merited so many tribulations and so
much resistance. Burney herself expressed dislike over those "name-
compelling" wills, making this issue the center of a critical debate
between Cecilia, Mrs. Delvile, and her son.[2] The conflict of tradition, represented by the Delvile family, versus individual desire,
represented by Mortimer and Cecilia, arises over the question of
whose name the couple will take. If Delvile takes the Beverley name,
his ancient patronym dies out; if Cecilia takes Delvile's name, she
loses her fortune. In spite of the fact that the heiress possesses social
status, independence, and "intelligence of mind," *Cecilia* exacerbates
the problem implicit in the relationship between name and economic
worth raised in *Evelina*. After the scene that Burney intended to be
pivotal, the heroine's tribulations cause her to go mad; both what
she inherits patrilineally and what she inherits in terms of patriarchal
discourse become obstacles to her memory and wholeness of mind.

Based on Foucault's history of madness, this chapter will explore
how the irrational, as described in *Cecilia,* indirectly gives a voice

to one who is otherwise culturally silenced. It will show that when woman is denied both speech *and* action her only access to a rational mind is also denied. Memory gives significance to the past by connecting, as Burney the diarist did, life's "strange medley of Thoughts and Facts" into a cultural narrative. When Cecilia loses her name, memory, and rational mind, she loses her signifiability in the memory of her culture. Unlike Evelina, she does not even write, that is, constitutively shape herself in her own memoirs.

Ordinarily memoirs are autobiographical, but in Burney's second work, subtitled "Memoirs of an Heiress," she abandons both the epistolary and the pretense of editor in favor of a narrative that sacrifices the freshness and immediacy of *Evelina* for a preconceived schema or "plot" and a more nominalized prose. The heiress not only loses her memory through madness but also loses her memoirs to an authoritative narrator who speaks, remembers, and "signifies" for her. The omniscient narrative voice only compounds rather than clarifies the problem of woman's trying to say herself.

Burke and Johnson praised *Cecilia* effusively—especially Burney's characters and "stock of observation" concerning human nature.[3] Mrs. Thrale, however, compared the novel unfavorably to Richardson's *Clarissa*. In describing *Cecilia* as a "Picture of Life such as the Author sees it," Mrs. Thrale may have unwittingly put her finger upon the crucial difference between female "scribbling" and patriarchal "authoring." Whereas the former sees the nexus of life and person as an open possibility, the latter places character within the boundary of the frame, the "Picture of Life," which the "Author" represents. Thus, Burney distances us from the immediate fabric of the novel's fictional world and instead calls attention to the authorizing voice of the narrator-author. Cecilia must communicate through a narration linked to an ideological order and established upon the silencing of woman. This discourse of Reason will be better understood when we develop its relation to madness.

The "gentle and amiable" Cecilia, in whose disposition "sweetness was tempered with dignity, and gentleness with fortitude," (3) possesses "a strong sense of DUTY, a fervent desire to ACT RIGHT" as "the ruling characteristics of her mind." "Good sense" plus "the rectitude of her heart and the soundness of her judgment" guard her "both from error and blame" but not from the madness that the privileging of the rational mind creates. This form of mad rationality is a kind of blindness and helps to explain the meaning of the name "Cecilia" as the "blind."

"Perfect sanity of mind," as Annie Raine Ellis notes in the 1882 preface to the novel, unites the virtue shared by the hero and heroine (xi). Certainly, Cecilia manifests the spirit that this novel embodies, specifically, the degree of discriminating sensibility that inhibits spontaneity with the caution of sense, or the sanity that Cecilia's world calls "delicacy." Nonetheless, for all the characters in the novel— from the punctiliously virtuous to the rapaciously villainous, from the judicious to the impulsive—the passions reign and, whether base or exalted, rule over actions.

"Human nature can rise no higher! . . . you are its most perfect ornament," says young Delvile of Cecilia (1:412). As a more dignified, grown-up version of Evelina, Cecilia is a "young woman of delicacy" who proceeds through life carefully by following the principles of an upright mind. As thoughtful as she is, Cecilia carefully tests all her notions by experience. The narrator describes her balanced comportment: "Her life was neither public nor private, her amusements were neither dissipated nor retired; the company she saw were either people of high rank or strong parts, and their visits were neither frequent nor long" (1:232).

Accordingly, Cecilia's admirers (among whom is the proud but estimable Mrs. Delvile) laud her for exemplifying the perfect balance of female traits: "So open to reason, so ingenuous in error! so rational! so just! so feeling, yet so wise!" (2:190). Others, like the wildly outspoken Albany, exhort, indeed demand, that she generously bestow her fortune upon the needy. Unlike Evelina, and notwithstanding these benevolist assaults, Cecilia has little of that form of self-deceiving naïveté that could precipitate her woes; she carefully observes others, never acts rashly, takes advice readily, and is "studiously cautious in avoiding all appearances that might strengthen" any whisper of impropriety (1:220). This sanity of mind is amply demonstrated in those situations where her behavior strongly contrasts with that of those who favor their own passions; the first volume of the novel concentrates on those episodes. For that reason, the three guardians chosen to watch over Cecilia and her fortune demonstrate that their passion is not a sane and sensible concern for their ward's well-being, but a selfish desire to keep her inheritance in the hands of proper male control. Each of the guardians is bent upon finding her a husband in order to preserve her fortune for male dominion—which in the case of Mr. Harrel means robbing her of the fortune for himself. Furthermore, each of the guardians assumes the superiority of *his* reason for preserving her best interests by inferring that *her* reason is mere female caprice. Exposed to schemes deliberately appealing to her tender heart and complications that would tax the most acute judgment, Cecilia manages to display an understanding beyond her years and experience. Even when yielding her money according to her personal sense of rightness, she displays a "sanity" far beyond that of her guardians.

Clearly, Burney takes pains to convince us that *only* Cecilia's upright mind guards her from the designs of the guardians that she inherits. She urges upon us a Cecilia who eludes the various snares laid for her by Mr. Harrel, skirts the caprices of Mr. Briggs, and overlooks the affronts of Mr. Delvile. Nonetheless, Burney also presses us to see Cecilia prudentially withholding herself when her own affections are not engaged. However, she can't foil as easily the designs upon her name and hence her ability to name.

Notwithstanding her triumph over such reason as her guardians provide, Cecilia finds her "fancies" more severely tried in the second half of the novel when her own passion is engaged by "a sympathy of sentiment so striking" for young Delvile:

> Her mind was now occupied . . . with an involuntary admiration . . . and felt for him a rising partiality. . . . Yet, . . . as her passions were under the control of her reason, and she suffered not her affections to triumph over her principles, she started at her danger the moment she perceived it, and instantly determined to give no weak encouragement to a prepossession. . . . She denied herself the deluding satisfaction of dwelling upon the supposition of his worth . . . that her heart might have less leisure for imagination; and had she found that his character degenerated from the promise of his appearance, the well regulated purity of her mind would soon have enabled her to have driven him wholly from her thoughts. (1:243–44)

Passions "under the control" of reason, principles in charge of affections, Cecilia denies herself "deluding satisfaction" and "leisure

for imagination." She vigilantly guards against the danger of "pre-
possession." Apparently the mind occupied with "involuntary admiration" signals the invasion of thought by affective prejudice; yet
when Delvile's "appearance" corresponds to his real character, the
"well regulated" mind drives such rationally perspicuous judgments
from it. Not surprisingly, such assiduous efforts to *deny* her own
reasoned reasoning, to thwart what her discursive thinking has prov-
en to be true—such efforts create the very condition for an "altered
state of mind" toward Delvile. Nevertheless, "this loss of mental
freedom gave her not much uneasiness, since the choice of her heart,
though involuntary, was approved by her principles, and confirmed
by her judgment" (1:245).

Confirmed in her judgment, Cecilia loves Delvile within the acceptable bounds of rational delicacy. Inexplicably, however, she receives no encouragement from young Delvile in spite of their mutual
attraction, so that "she determined to conquer her partiality" (1:255).
When Delvile finally blurts out his regard, Cecilia is pleased that
his struggles to contain himself "were proofs just such as she wished
to receive . . . which assured her that her own secret was still sacred,
and that no weakness or inadvertency on her part had robbed her
of the power of . . . dignity" (1:302). Even in the throes of love, Cecilia
remains decorously—even proudly—judicious.

Certainly if rewards could be meted out for female conduct,
Cecilia merits her nobleman, especially since she has consistently
reflected upon her actions "by the severest examination of her own
conduct" (2:184). Rebuffed, "her conduct, seldom equal to her notions of right, . . . the reproaches of her judgment," enable her to
forget her affliction (2:184–85). Once again, even when puzzled by
Delvile's ambiguous behavior "time and constancy of mind soon
lessened its difficulty" for Cecilia (2:4).

Cecilia soon discovers that the unusual condition under which she
inherits her fortune (the patrilineal name passing on through her to
her husband) is the *real* obstacle to her marriage and reason for her
rejection: "—the change of name is the obstacle; he inherits all the
pride of his family, —and therefore to that family will I unrepining
leave him!" (2:55). The passionate Delvile confesses his love with
regret that he cannot, by giving up his name, take hers, because,
"*my* honour in the honour of my family is bound" (2:56). Yet even
in *this* most difficult moment, she resigns herself to her loss. The

narrator explains that "resolution, in such cases, may act the office of time, and anticipate by reason and self-denial, what that, much less nobly, effects through forgetfulness and inconstancy" (2:80). The irony of Burney's words will become apparent when Cecilia's "forgetfulness" and Delvile's "inconstancy" effect the actual resolution.

Her resolution is short-lived; impetuous Delvile convinces her to elope and avoid the refusal of his family. He insists that there is no argument to be "offered by reason, to notions that exist but by prejudice." The marriage, interrupted and aborted, confirms Cecilia's own prior misgivings: "None of our proceedings have prospered, . . . their privacy has always been contrary both to my judgment and my principles" (2:169). The scene is now set for the point in the narrative toward which Burney said *Cecilia* was intended (vii).

The Delviles, like the guardians, are guided by their passion when appealing to Cecilia's sanity—a form of reason which they passionately insist must abjure feeling. When Mrs. Delvile eloquently begs Cecilia to renounce her son, she repeatedly appeals to Cecilia's mind, which could "never err with impunity" but could be "pre-occupied [*sic*] with an intention to be guided by the dictates of inclination" (2:177). Cecilia insists, "My mind harbours no such intention, it has no desire but to be guided by duty" (2:177). Representing the cultural hegemony of her family's "common voice, common opinion, and common address," Mrs. Delvile asserts that her son is the "sole guardian of its name" and its only heir (2:178). As worthy as Cecilia may be, patronymic codes lay prior claim to that of love and supersede the name Cecilia borrows from her family:

> They assert their rights with the authority of prescription, they forbid us alike either to bend to inclination, or stoop to interest, . . . their injuries will call out for redress, should their noble and long unsullied name be voluntarily assigned to oblivion. (2:179)

It is important to note that only under the patriarchal "rights with the authority of prescription" can Mrs. Delvile wield so forceful a claim upon Cecilia's mind. Burney skillfully handles the strong, indeed the extreme, passion with which Mrs. Delvile couches her appeal of reason, which neither purports to "bend to inclination" nor to "stoop to interest." She is equally as dexterous when describing Cecilia's feelings, "almost bursting with conflicting passions," that

alternate between showing her offended pride and her disappointed
tenderness. Seeing that she has gained her point, Mrs. Delvile names
Cecilia "daughter of my mind! So open to reason . . . so rational!
so just! so feeling, yet so wise!" (2:190). Hence, her appeal and
appellation, "daughter of my mind" proclaim a particular female
kinship in which passion must take the appearance of self-sacrifice
in order to be deemed a mind. This kinship recognizes by its denial
of passion the power inherent in such a passionate appeal to reason.
Those who inherit a name only in marriage become champions of
the very process that disinherits them.

In marked contrast, Delvile, with "emotion far more violent,
because wholly unrestrained," acts "under the influence of such
irrational violence" (2:211); Cecilia, by comparison, remains quiet
and, at least outwardly, self-possessed. Mrs. Delvile, chastising her
son, explains to Cecilia that he is "a young man who passionately
adores you" with "a passion built on such a defalcation of principle"
that it "renders him unworthy your acceptance" (2:212). Cecilia,
though for the most part remaining silent, again repeats her renunciation—to which both of the Delviles offer their praise. From
Mrs. Delvile:

> *You* cannot be unhappy, you have purchased peace by the exercise
> of virtue, and the close of every day will bring to you a reward,
> in the sweets of a self-approving mind. (2:213)

And from Delvile, "her greatness of mind is like your own." Thus,
their appeal to Cecilia's rationality via the "sweets of a self-approving
mind" is one *of* passion concealed by various "reasons" *to* passion.
Accordingly, Mrs. Delvile can, by "the passions with which she was
agitated," fault her son when saying that he is "blinded" by passion,
his "nobler feelings" obscured (2:215). He can retort that *her* intention
is to work, not upon the reason, but "upon the feelings of Miss
Beverley." As we have seen, however, for Cecilia a self-approving
mind is one in which "a strong sense of duty," the "fervent desire
to act right," is the ruling passion—ruling but unable to accommodate her equally strong feelings for Delvile. If we recall that
Cecilia has insisted that a fervent desire to do right is the *only*
inclination of her mind, then we can already see that her definition
of the upright mind does not merely suppress passion—it denies it.

What becomes even more apparent, however, is that all of the characters reveal in their actions the passion with which they are motivated to appeal to the norm of the rational.

Delvile finally admits he has been "impetuous, violent, unreasonable" and that he has persecuted, reproached, and censured that "very dignity of conduct which has been the basis of my admiration, my esteem, my devotion!" (2:222, 223). After some further entanglements, and with considerable reservations on Cecilia's part, she and Delvile marry. Consenting to a clandestine marriage, in which she "voluntarily assigns her name to oblivion" by yielding up her fortune, brings her no immediate happiness; Cecilia feels herself:

> Suffering [i.e., allowing] the whole peace of her future life to hang upon an action, dark, private, and imprudent: an action by which the liberal kindness of her late uncle would be annulled, by which the father of her intended husband would be disobeyed, and which already, in a similar instance, had brought her to affliction and disgrace. (2:362, 363)

Marriage robs her of her name, her fortune, and most of all, her peace. Her dilemma recalls Simone de Beauvoir's claim that the husband is the one who goes beyond family interest out into society, thereby participating in the collective destiny of his culture. The female, on the other hand, is allowed no direct influence upon the future; she reaches society indirectly, as a nurturer and through the authority and mediation of her husband.[4] His discursive authority categorially confines even her speech. For example, Delvile can declare his affections, coerce Cecilia into a secret marriage, declaim his passion, and still seem manly and rational. Cecilia can neither declare her feelings nor assert her desires; she can neither act upon her reason nor accept the strength of her passion. In adopting the dominant mode of reason she submits to an absolute rectitude antithetical to feeling. "Sanity of mind," her highest principle, prevents her from forgiving herself. Truth, publicly understood as discursive reasoning, prevents her from speaking truly of her own passion. When she cannot redeem herself in language, she must borrow from silence a different kind of voice.

Further complicating matters, Mr. Delvile refuses to grant the harassed young wife refuge. The nearly incoherent Cecilia finds these latest trials so overwhelming that "grief and horror for what was past, apprehension and suspense for what was to come, so disordered her whole frame, so confused even her intellects [*sic*] . . . she sat . . . silent, quiet, and erect, almost vacant of all thought, yet with a secret idea she was doing something right" (2:386). Later, when Cecilia goes mad, the narrator will inform us that Delvile, the elder patriarch, is the "author of this scene of woe" (2:444).

So far we can see how narrative events contrast Cecilia's sanity of mind with the eccentricities of those who, under the guise of reason, are ruled by passion. We can also see that "upright mind" for a female describes only those sacrificial actions expressed by aiding both friends and the needy, bearing cruel affronts passively, and following the advice of her peers. There does seem to be a discrepancy, however, between the reason that appeals to the logic of correct judgment and that which merely masks the desires of others—as both the actions of her guardians and that of the Delviles demonstrate. What she and others regard as unreasonable in her is *any* act that promotes her own self-interest, though when the Delviles promote *their* own interests both they and she tend to accept that act as "reasonable." When she upholds the female standard of benevolence and self-sacrifice, she abuses that of reason, and indirectly contradicts her exercise of judgment. Included in this contradiction is an opposition between reason and passion that assumes strong feelings *must* be both distinguished from and subjugated to reason— a difference in which Cecilia *must* exclude passion from reason in order to be considered reasonable. It is this ruling order of reason that imposes a standard of benevolent caring as the only acceptable contour for female passion. The sole dress a woman's passion can wear and still be held rational disguises personal desire, disguises it in the transparency of sincerity and care. It is no wonder, then, that at an earlier masked ball, Cecilia is the only one of the main characters not appearing in disguise. Dressed in the sincerity of selflessness without guile, she excludes the vulgar accoutrement of personal desire—and excludes it in the name of reason.

Cecilia defers to the sensibleness of what may reasonably be expected in life rather than what feeds one's own hopes and desires— that deference contrasts the self-serving behavior of everyone else in the novel. The others passionately cling to the "dangerous prevalence of the imagination," despite the plausibility of experience. They are directed by their passions and desires to rationalize their actions. Dr. Lyster attests to this activity: "The whole of this unfortunate business . . . has been the result of PRIDE and PREJUDICE" (2:462). He links the right of patrilineal name to willfulness when he points out to Cecilia that her conflict is due to the "humours" of Mr. Delvile and those of Cecilia's uncle, who "was just as fond of his name." Thus, the underlying issue of name takes on added import, for it is a passion for possessing name that authors the scene of madness and defines reason in terms of those who bear the "name of the father."

Although Cecilia constantly tries to balance the opposition between her desires and her reason, her efforts are thwarted by those who insist that the legitimate use of reason belongs to those named in authority, the patriarchal. As long as Cecilia held the borrowed right to the patrilineal name (the rule of order upon which name is based), she could properly exercise that right to reason. But when she assigns her name to oblivion by taking that of Delvile, she forfeits that right. Her legitimacy, that is, any claim she may have to assert her own desire as reasonable, is subverted by the reigning authority of reason (under the guise of passion) represented by the patronymic name and succession of Delvile. Her only rational choice seems to be to bear evil (Delvile, devil, evil ?) with feminine resignation: "Rationally, however, she surveyed the world at large, and finding that of the few who had any happiness, there were none without some misery, she checked the rising sigh of repining mortality, and, grateful with general felicity, bore partial evil with cheerfullest resignation" (2:473). Cruelly rebuffed by Mr. Delvile in spite of her request—"I beseech him not to refuse me! tell him I have something to communicate that requires his immediate attention"—distressed by Delvile's jealousy—"he was in a great passion, and would hardly hear anything"—Cecilia vainly tries to find her husband. Horrified at finding herself even without shelter, the rational Cecilia, perceived by herself and others as calm, steady, and reserved, becomes blind to all but her passion and goes mad with delirium. The form of her blindness and the discourse of her madness become crucial for understanding the ruling order of Reason.

Since Cecilia's right to her own name, paradigmatic of woman's inheritance, is "voluntarily assigned to oblivion," she loses her memory, her mind, and her ability to give significance to her past and future. The narrator-analyst (who takes over her memoirs) describes this point in a passage that is *both* the discourse of reason *and* the cry of madness:

> This moment, for the unhappy Cecilia, teemed with calamity; she was wholly overpowered; terror for Delvile, horror for herself, hurry, confusion, heat and fatigue, all assailing her at once, while all means of repelling them were denied her, the attack was too strong for her fears, feelings, and faculties, and her reason suddenly, yet totally failing her, she madly called out, 'He will be gone! he will be gone! and I must follow him to Nice!'(2:428–29)

Reason forbidden its prior attunement in desires, fears, and feelings will not recognize, and therefore cannot repel, an attack of its own kind: the reason that the patriarchy uses to deny woman a hearing robs her of understanding.

Though Cecilia's memoirs are displaced from her own memory to that of the narrative voice, she is bereft of more than memories by the conceptual thinking that robs her of mind. Before assigning causes to her madness, we need to explore the changing symptoms of madness, symptoms not simply limited to the diagnosis of psychopathology that permanently places madness in the realm outside the discourse of truth.

Michel Foucault says in the preface to *Madness and Civilization: A History of Insanity in the Age of Reason*:

> We must try to return, in history, to that zero point in the course of madness at which madness is an undifferentiated experience, a not yet divided experience of division itself. . . . What is constitutive is the action that divides madness, and not the science elaborated once this division is made and calm restored. What is originative is the caesura that establishes the distance between reason and non-reason; reason's subjugation of non-reason, wresting from it its truth as madness, crime, or disease, derives explicitly from this point. . . . Then, and then only, can we determine the realm in which the man of madness and the man of reason, moving apart, are not yet disjunct.[5]

Foucault says that before the classical age of reason, madness was a kind of truth that acknowledged mystery, but that after the Renaissance, "the experience of madness remains silent in the composure of a knowledge which, knowing too much about madness, forgets it" (*MC,* xii). This point of disjunction is precisely what *Cecilia* discloses, the zero point at which reason and unreason diverge into patriarchical civilization ("man of reason") and the feminine other ("man [*sic*] of madness"). That is, when truth becomes correspondence with some norm, correctness as measured by "Nature," then madness or "unreason" becomes error and the discourse of the irrational, female hysteric under the science of psychology. To account for Cecilia's madness simply by saying that it expresses a denied self-determination obscures the important change in the entire history of the way a culture determines madness, and thereby, understands alterity. It is also conceptually naive—perhaps a form of madness—to adopt the very model of self-determination that the patriarchy champions and uses to constrain women, as well as the mad.

This extraordinary turn in the plot of *Cecilia* becomes explicable in light of Foucault's description of the historical moment when madness (or unreason) ceases to exist alongside reason and becomes conceptualized as the "other" of rationality (or irrationality). The *plot* of this novel *is* that moment, and Cecilia's madness reveals the concealed dynamics of reason *and* unreason narrowed to rationality *or* irrationality. As Barbara Hill Rigney points out, madness is a "political event" which, "to a greater or lesser degree, is connected to the female social condition."[6] That female social condition inheres in the dualism reason-madness. It becomes public or political when the cultural destiny of woman, alien other of the male, the threat of the irrational that is felt to necessitate the dominion of rationality and the subjugation of alterity, adopts a new guise: the ultimate competent analysis and diagnosis of madness (psychoanalysis). While Foucault's own analysis of madness does not include the gendering of madness as feminine, Burney's does. Her analysis shows how the eighteenth century often equates that competent diagnosis of feminine madness with the objectivity of the patriarchal authorial voice.

And what is the comportment of Cecilia's madness? She refuses to listen to male advice and forcibly disengages herself from her persecuters (2:429). She forgets her "situation, her intention, and herself." She escapes both "pursuit and insult" by the "velocity of her own motion." In her delirium, Cecilia can at last speak of her personal anguish and her own passion outside the rule of reason. Burney describes Cecilia as forced "along by her own vehement rapidity, not hearing what was said, not heeding what was thought" (2:430). Hence, Cecilia no longer hears or regards the discourse that socially and politically constructs a persona by constricting her feelings and desires. When she collapses inside a pawnshop, the spectators account for her by supposing she broke out of Bedlam. Cecilia protests, "No, no,—I am not mad,—I am going to Nice—to my husband," but the words alone do not prove her rational, for her behavior and the circumstances of the situation convince the others, in spite of her words, that she is irrational, since "she could give no account who she was, whence she came, or whither she wished to go" (2:431). The condition of an improper identity—lack of inheritance, lack of name, lack of significance to cultural memory— is also the comportment of madness and is gendered feminine.

Because Cecilia behaves in a manner outside the acceptable norm, others assume she is irrational. Nonetheless, they judge her by more than a reified conceptual structure limited to verbal statements. They understand her madness according to a radical manifoldness of interpretation that undermines Reason even when their action causes her anguish: "She found herself shut up in a place of confinement, without light, without knowledge where she was, and not a human being near her!" (2:431).[7] Because reason struggles to assert itself over and against unreason manifested as all that is negative, "confinement is the practice which corresponds most exactly to madness experienced as unreason, that is, as the empty negativity of reason; by confinement, madness is acknowledged to be *nothing*" (*MC,* 116). "Nothing," as Alice Jardine points out, is usually configured as woman.[8] A conceptual wall between madness and sanity keeps madness under control until it "comes to its senses."

At first, Cecilia's delirious discourse is coherent. Her passion cannot speak, however, because it would violate her as a "pattern of all goodness." Cecilia finds that when the passions are no longer one among many of the causes of madness, but are instead the means for madness to penetrate reason, and, thereby, a reason for passions to be suppressed, the notion of the "upright" mind that she tried to uphold becomes a kind of insanity. Consequently, madness liberates her passions from their limits, liberates her speech from cultural prohibition, and liberates her thinking from the tyranny of reason. Madness conceals, guards as it were, her passion and desires from the suppression of reason. Burney says that in madness Cecilia's "fancy roved." Once judged to be mad, Cecilia's cries are ignored because the discourse of madness, no longer human, has no means of connecting with that of reason: "Mrs. Wyers . . . sought no longer to draw from her . . . who she was . . . fully persuaded that her case was that of decided insanity . . . " (2:432). When assuming Cecilia's nonbeing, Mrs. Wyers acts consistently, since those held to be mad in an age of reason are considered nonhuman, and therefore, feminine.

The following advertisement is placed in the paper: "MADNESS / Whereas a crazy young lady . . . ran into the Three Blue Balls . . . [she] has been kept there since out of charity." The omniscient narrator, another voice representing the order of reason, tells us that Cecilia "raves" for two days and two nights without food or water: "And thus, though naturally and commonly of a silent and quiet disposition, she was now not a moment still, for the irregular starts of a terrified and disordered imagination were changed into the constant ravings of morbid delirium" (2:433). The nature of these ravings is yet to be explored.

In the chapter entitled "Passion and Delirium," Foucault says that "the ultimate language of madness is that of reason" (95). He adds that delirious language is the discourse that liberates passion from all its limits, that firmly adheres to reason while departing from it. In other words, madness, as manifested in delirious discourse, is an error in which the mad(wo)man deceives herself; consequently, the madman no longer understands the true according to the standard of correctness and the false according to that of error (101, 107). Foucault's history describes the standard for truth in the age of reason: that one *can* tell the true from the false, that truth can be ultimately verifiable and obey the rules of a world fully and veridically given. When events fail to make the sense to Cecilia that they should, the sense of the veridical, her reason fails—but another kind of reason takes its place.

Cecilia's delirious discourse concentrates upon an image, a need to rescue Delvile that blinds her to all else: "Senses wholly disorderd; she forgot her situation, her intention, and herself; the single idea of Delvile's danger took sole possession of her brain, though all connection with its occasion was lost" (2:429). In losing her senses,

she is blind; in concentrating only upon the idea in her mind, she
loses touch with the immediate (present), forgetting her situation
(past), her intention (future), and herself (an ecstasis of past, present,
future). Thus Burney shows us that woman's inheritance is an am-
nesia of memory, rational mind, and name.

It is not that Cecilia's words don't make sense; nor is it that her
madness bespeaks the revered fragility of reason as might have been
true in an earlier era when, for example, Pascal can speak of a
logique du cœur. Cecilia's situation is that *her* reason does not correspond to the prevailing reason of representation. As Foucault notes,
in madness there is not a specific change in mind or in body so
much as the existence of a conduct of delirious discourse (100); thus,
an image, and therefore an illusion, "took such full possession of
her senses." Blinded by her hallucination to everything else, this
form of blindness Foucault calls "the culmination of the void" (107).

Foucault's description of madness and the void has a counterpart
in a work from the eighteenth century. It is in the famous chapter
entitled "The Dangerous Prevalence of Imagination" in Johnson's
Rasselas that Imlac says:

> Disorders of intellect . . . happen much more often than . . . ob-
> servers will easily believe. . . . There is no man whose imagination
> does not sometimes predominate over his reason, who can regulate
> his attention wholly by his will, and whose ideas will come and
> go at his command. . . . All power of fancy over reason is a degree
> of insanity . . . it is not visible to others . . . it is not pronounced
> madness but when it comes ungovernable, and apparently influ-
> ences speech or action. (693–94)

Imlac describes the telos that imagination fixes upon as an answer
to desire which narrows passion to an object of desire, so that the
possibility of madness can be implicit in the phenomenon of any
passion. The narrowing of passion to an object of desire, such as
the desire for the rational mind, evacuates from understanding all
those human concerns assigned by the rule of order to chaos, the
ungovernable, or what Foucault calls, the void.

As woman, Cecilia's discourse is provisional, and strains the
boundaries of rational discourse, threatening at any moment to spill
over into the chaos of non-reason. Those who analyze and listen to

her delirium, even though it is coherent, are already persuaded "that her case was that of decided insanity, and had not any notion of temporary or accidental alienation of reason" (2:432). We are reminded of Julia Kristeva's claim that woman's discourse is peripheral, that is, consigned to the margins of discourse.[9] Disrupting the linguistic system that prevails, however, introduces the marginal into that system. A female's discourse of madness, then, would make audible a voice that has been relegated to the blank spaces, to the void. To be heard, the language of affects, Cecilia's "terror" and "horror," must pass from affect to conceptual language. To enter into the social order that normally prohibits a woman from speaking her desires, her feelings, and her sense of who she is—she must either adopt the prevailing discourse as her own, thereby disobeying the prohibition against woman's speaking, or she must speak in a manner that is unintelligible to the public world and interpretable only as madness. To let someone else speak for her and call her irrational or for her to speak for herself and be interpreted as mad are the two alternatives of the double bind of representational discourse (Reason). Fixing the limits of discourse ensures how one will be identified within it. Any step over the boundary set for defining the individual is censured: "The classical mind condemned in madness a certain blindness to the truth . . . which exceeds the juridical limits of the individual, ignores the moral limits fixed for . . . [her], and tends to an apotheosis of the self" (*MC*, 264). By concealing herself under the guise of madness, a guise that the prevailing discourse can *only* interpret as madness, Cecilia at last gives voice to her desire.

Unlike Evelina whose lack of self-awareness causes her to adopt a course of action that covers over her desires and rationalizes her feelings, Cecilia assents to an attitude toward the rational that denies her the right to personal feelings and desires that serve her own interest. Just as Cecilia believes in Delvile's prerogative to be her authority, so she also believes that the authority of Reason stands in the place of her desires and feelings. Because Cecilia grants the upright mind final authority to examine and judge her every emotion, she is disturbed when she can find no rational reasons to justify her feelings. She cannot justify them because woman, as a repository of virtue ("pattern of all goodness"), finds it her virtuous, feminine duty to surrender her feelings and desires to the desires of others.

Furthermore, because the model of intellect excludes desire and feeling from the field of its own activity, Cecilia finds no space for her desires *within* rational discourse. That is, she cannot find a discourse, a "consoling myth" that answers to her needs, that speaks for her, that discloses meaning for her in the chaos of her experience. Cecilia cries wildly that "no one will save me now! I am married and no one will listen to me!" (2:435). The "angel in the house," the one who gives advice and consolation, the one who listens, smiles and sympathizes, must surrender her personal comfort and desire or be held a "monster."[10]

If Delvile acknowledged Cecilia publicly as his bride, she would have the right to speak her mind, to represent her new family name. Like Evelina, however, Cecilia has no authority to speak unless she borrows the authority of her husband who "authors" her. Because Delvile has not granted her this authority by acknowledging her as his wife, she finds "no one will listen to me!" If she had her husband's guardianship, and by right, that of his father (the inherited rights of the community), she might speak to him "all that was on her heart." In madness, Cecilia's stern resolution shows "a stubbornness, wholly foreign to her genuine character" because the strength of her desires and feelings are outside the realm that circumscribes her "genuine character" (2:437).

Within the plot of this novel, Burney reveals the plotting calculation underlying any authoritative ordering of action: Cecilia's madness demonstrates that the irrational rules unnoticed and hidden in the rational. Just as Burney the diarist discovered that "whimsical," "flighty" and "half-mad" thoughts in a "strange medley" were the enabling condition, the possibility for "self," so in abandoning the episodic for plot, she discovers that an attempt to master identity by structuring it is self-disintegrative. Burney reveals, in other words, the dominant structure of thought—plotting *is* the order of madness.

In a reversal of patriarchal roles and blinded by her own form of reason Cecilia does not recognize who Delvile is. He exclaims against Cecilia's justice, "Is then Delvile utterly renounced? . . . do you deny him even a place in your remembrance?" He asks, "Is it me or my name you thus disown?" Cecilia's answer that "once I loved it . . . when I was cold and wretched, I cherished it; and when I was abandoned and left alone, I repeated it and sung to it"—that response prompts Delvile's conclusion that "her reason is utterly gone"

(2:439). This is the irony that Chesterton noted when he said there is a particular kind of madness that consists in losing everything *but* one's reason. The truth revealed in Cecilia's madness is that the rational is irrational and, as the irrational, is a kind of madness.

The rhetorical movement for Cecilia is one from defeat in the rational to protection in madness: "Cecilia resisted them . . . imploring them not to bury her alive, and averring . . . they meant to entomb her" (2:440). And at last she takes refuge in muteness. Yielding to the inexpressible, she escapes the bonds of plot, the linear and the logical. Madness enables her language to lose the authority of rational statement and its rule-governed structure. After Cecilia "raves," she falls into an "unconscious state." Then "wholly insensible, but perfectly quiet; she seemed to distinguish nothing, and neither spoke nor moved" (2:444). As one whose role is that of a sacrificial nurturer, Cecilia is "heard" only when her discourse provides affective maintenance. Albany asks, "Wilt thou not speak?" "She can't sir," said one of the women; "she has been speechless many hours" (2:448). In one of the most horrifically ironic lines in the novel he declares, "*Her mouth was never opened but to give comfort*" (2:449, emphasis added). Unwittingly he underscores how woman's discourse will be accepted as reasonable only if she opens her mouth to give comfort.

When Delvile finds her, he is terrified. Sure that he will "mangle and destroy" her, he would rather she died than that he "bear the sound of so lovely a voice uttering nothing." Meanwhile, the elder Delvile is filled with self-recrimination from the pangs "which called him author of this scene of woe." Cecilia becomes feverish and succumbs to "incoherent ravings," then silence, and at last, the blindness of sleep. Yet, even awake Cecilia is blind to herself. With the world in view, she gives comfort and care but remains blind to her own desires. When both speech and action are denied her, her access to even a provisional identity is denied. Conversely, when she is blind to the world in her madness, seeing only the images of her own mind, she is also denied both the speech and action that would distinguish her and grant her worldly citizenship. The world silences her in forcing her to speak only in the discourse of benevolent sacrifice. Her private discourse embodies the spontaneous shape of *her* desires but does not connect with the dominant public discourse of reason.

The mad Cecilia vividly demonstrates how the community interprets her on the basis of a nonverbal fabric—her gestures, facial
expression, clothes, circumstance—a fabric that does not include any
verbal significance provided by Cecilia herself. That is, Cecilia's
madness reveals how ruthlessly the discourse of reason excludes the
value of female speech when it denies the nonverbal texture with
which *it* interprets the world. The gap in discourse created by madness speaks a mythic paradigm about woman's silence and suffering,
about her patriarchally incited hysteria. With Cecilia unconscious,
Dr. Lyster, Delvile, Henrietta, and Albany all speak for her; when
she awakens, her "intellects restored," and speaks for herself—the
world is different.

Cecilia's madness changes her world because as one who is mad,
she *is* heard. She acts the forbidden within the public and transforms
her silence, a sign of her negation, into action. This action is a new
beginning in the sense of instituting a series of unpredictable events.
Her madness becomes an action that creates a space for another
voice in an otherwise univocal world.[11]

Though Patricia Spacks correctly notes that Cecilia "must use
her energies for self-suppression" and that this suppression diminishes her character,[12] one must not confuse self-suppression with
repression of the symbolic function. Cecilia cannot act when she
cannot understand the preconceived narrative, or plot, that is sup-
posed to lend coherence to her desire. Her discourse of delirium is
one of those revolutions in poetic language that Kristeva says "does
not constitute the acknowledgment of the unconscious but is instead
its expenditure and implementation."[13] The story ends with the narrative voice telling us that "the strong spirit of active benevolence
which had ever marked her character, was now again displayed
though no longer, as hitherto, unbounded. . . . The upright mind of
Cecilia, her purity, her virtue, and the moderation of her wishes,
gave to her in the warm affection of Lady Delvile, and the unremitting fondness of Mortimer, all the happiness human life seems
capable of receiving" (2:471, 473). Although the disruptive discourse
of the irrational may no longer be "unbounded," it may be bound
to and by the ruling order of reason, so that the only legitimate
form of female desire lies within the constraints of "active benevolence." Yet, as Margaret Doody has pointed out, the novel abounds
with other mad characters who stretch the bounds of reason.[14] Hence,

the order of reason imposed upon the ending defines the boundaries of an entire *realm* of madness, a realm that Cecilia surveys "rationally," and bears "with cheerfullest resignation" (2:473).

Evelina thought she needed to learn prudence in order to maintain what she considered to be her essential innocence. In her letters she revealed to the reader, if not to herself, that the reflexive process of writing as an event of meaning was self-constitutive, whereas the model of female essence—a kind of plot imposed upon her—was self-destructive. Although Cecilia begins her story with the prudence and thoughtfulness that Evelina thinks she lacks, she nonetheless assumes, like Evelina, that the world is a container full of essences. The values of reason and female caring that she clings to seem incomprehensibly oppositional even though she ends her story with all her "intellects" and opinions intact. The question that needs to be asked is not whether her reasoning corresponds, but whether her self-configuration coheres. That is, do Cecilia's categories of reason and feeling offer a praxis for human being that takes account of woman?

In the "Letter on Humanism" Heidegger says: "Because we are speaking against 'logic' people believe that we are demanding that rigor of thinking be renounced and in its place the arbitrariness of drives and feelings be installed and thus that 'irrationalism' be proclaimed as true. For what is more 'logical' than that whoever speaks against the logical is defending the alogical?"[15] He goes on to describe how people assume the logic that what speaks against something is its negation, and that negation is destructive. When reasoning sees reason as an exact correspondence between two identities and posits in advance what is "positive," "irrationalism . . . rules unnoticed and uncontested in the defense of 'logic'" ("Letter," 227). The logic of Cecilia's madness forces the "rational" to take account of what it labels "irrational" and to allow language to speak the discourse of the other. Cecilia's madness, her lack of cultural memory and inheritance, forms a story told as memoirs; it restores to her a memory and an inheritance—though still under the ruling order of omniscient narrative, a ruling order that itself is explicitly exposed by Burney as the action of madness. Kristeva says, "The text is the active form of madness which breaks the signifying process out of its confines in the madness of the dominant discourse" (*Revolution*, 214).

The narrative stance Burney employs to tell Cecilia's memoirs seems to fail in bringing about the wholistic "temperance" of mind that it advocates. In *Cecilia*, Burney purportedly imitates Johnson in relying upon a style built on latinate nominalizations. Nominalizations turn verbs, action, the dynamics of process, into essences, nouns; they stop movement, they create the passive voice, they fix passage. Thus, Burney paints a "Picture of Life" filled with characters who are arrested, stilled in their acts by her own prose style, a style borrowed from those "Censors" and "Magistrates" of writing. The regulative order of reason goes far in explaining why a recognized, female, public author like Burney has little choice but to adopt the omnisicient authorial voice in her second novel. As she says in the original preface, "The indulgence shown by the public to *Evelina* ... unpatronized, unaided and unowned, ... has encouraged its Author to risk this *second* attempt." She writes not only to earn money, i.e., the original "Advertisement," but also to win approval from the critical and familial orderers of public novel reading. When an authorized narrative voice legislates female passion by imposing the standard of benevolent care upon the behavior of its heroine, the effect is often one of distance between Cecilia and the reader. Once again, someone else speaks for her. The discussion of the next novel will further explore the split between reason and feeling and show it to be inherently contradictory. Since the eighteenth century determines as opposites "rationality," correct to the nature of things, and "irrationality," captive to the sway of feeling, Burney will try to reconcile this opposition of identity and difference. Under the signs of male and female she assigns ultimate Authorial sovereignty to a feminine signatory: Queen Charlotte. Her solution becomes a part of the problem, however, as an all-sovereign female affectivity enjoins the power of representation to resist male reason.

3

Camilla: *The Heart Has Its Reasons*

Le cœur a ses raisons que la raison ne connaît point.
—Pascal

"HOW REPUGNANT TO SEVENTEEN is every idea of life that is rational."
This advice from the worldly-wise Mrs. Arlbery to Camilla in
Burney's third novel, subtitled "A Picture of Youth," is not without
its irony—especially when that same advice includes a description
of the "life that is rational" as "a solid connection [i.e., marriage]
formed with a view to the worldly comforts of existence" and hence
"really beneficial."[1] Since the insouciant Arlbery manages, within
the bounds of propriety created by this novel, to have her own way
and keep the admiration, indeed even the respect, of the decorous
world she moves in, her advice to the naive Camilla merits closer
scrutiny.

In the scene mentioned above, Arlbery realistically advises Camilla on the subject that Burney describes as the theme of her novel:
"The wilder wonders of the Heart of man; that amazing assemblage
of all possible contrarieties, in which one thing alone is steady—the
perverseness of spirit which grafts desire on what is denied" (7). If
contradiction is inherent in the "Heart of man" ("the heart has its
reasons which reason cannot know"), then we need to explore those
places in the novel that set up those opposing forces in discourse—
for those forces shape the two main characters and create their
conflict. In this her third novel, Burney abandons the balance and
judgment of a more mature Cecilia and turns instead to a female
character whose "imprudence," the Rev. Tyrold warns, "cannot but

53

end . . . [the] modest propriety . . . remarked as the attribute(s) of your character" (362). Similarly, she presents us with an opposing male character who has, in Dr. Johnson's words, the prudence that "keeps life safe, but does not often make it happy."[2] Camilla's impulsive artlessness and Edgar's tormenting doubt are mutually determining oppositions that exacerbate their errors: Arlbery says to Camilla, "You do not see, he does not, perhaps, himself know, how exactly he is calculated to make you wretched" (482).

Whereas the previous chapter explored the irrational in *Cecilia*, this chapter will describe what happens when the affective is displaced from what a particular culture regards as the rational. Accordingly, if a culture (both the novel and the social practices that produce it) expels the affective from its discourse, then *both* the depiction of the rational, as in the case of Edgar, and that of the affective, as in the case of Camilla, will reveal how desire is grafted on what is denied. In other words, the essential tension in the novel arises when a character of "melting sensibility" who rejects the rational falls in love with a "watcher" without trust who grafts desire on the very affectivity that his notion of the rational denies. The result of such a conflict is that both parties end up as victims of their culture. Burney summarizes this conflict when she says that *both* Edgar and Camilla "so nearly fell . . . sacrifice to the two extremes of Imprudence, and Suspicion, to the natural heedlessness of youth unguided, or to the acquired distrust of experience that had been wounded" (913). In order, then, effectively to explore the opposition of the affective ("Imprudence") and the rational ("Suspicion"), we need to discover how the context of the novel itself describes those conditions. To do so we will examine the kind of realistic advice that Mrs. Arlbery gives Camilla and contrast it to the rational advice Dr. Marchmont gives Edgar. In addition, we will take a close look at the sermon of Mr. Tyrold to see what the novel offers as the mean between these two rational views. When Burney charts the course of woman in *Camilla*, she places the female within an even more polarized context of gender than in the two earlier novels.

I

What are the questions to be asked of this novel? Edward and Lillian Bloom say in the introduction to *Camilla* that "from the very be-

ginning of composition, Fanny Burney meant *Camilla* . . . to exploit
the pathos of 'the tender sympathy'."[3] If we recall that Burney worked
under financial duress—she had to support her family, avoid rapacious booksellers, and please a public which favored a "crying
volume"—we can see how exchange value can subvert aesthetic
value.[4] This particular version of "tender sympathy" is entangled
with the economic pressures on Burney. The dichotomy between a
public, economic sphere and a private, "feminized" sphere is ex-
acerbated when a female writer grafts a private pattern of affectivity
onto a public system of "success." This issue, already embryonic in
the early diaries, will develop when Burney later thematizes "female
difficulties" in *The Wanderer*.

Feminist commentary has pointed out how equating women with
the "delicate sensibilities" denigrates female affectivity and strips
women of a resource for finding meaningful satisfaction in their
limited lives.[5] Women may find practical reasons for developing,
even exploiting, their affectivity (as Mrs. Arlbery suggests to Camilla), since, as Rose Marie Cutting says, women must undergo a
process of socialization that requires certain affective displays in order
to merit a husband and the right of social integration.[6] At the same
time, however, they must also appear prudent, not overly impulsive,
or else risk censure. Certainly the "delicate sensibilities" are not
traits that enable one to act assertively or even rationally for that
matter—especially if to do so threatens one's acceptance and rep-
utation in the community.

In a similar vein, the view that a female provides "affective maintenance" can quickly degenerate into an obligation, duty, even law.
When she is forced into a role of giving and pleasing, a woman
cannot articulate her needs so that others are unaware of them.[7]
Affective maintenance, what most moralists at the time described as
a woman's chief characteristic, was also regarded by them as pro-
foundly ambivalent, says Mary Poovey in her book *The Proper Lady
and the Woman Writer*.[8] A woman's affective comportment considered
as "amiableness of disposition" was assumed to form the basis of a
woman's "benevolence," her "sprightliness of imagination," and her
"sensibility of heart" (18).

The inability of an eighteenth-century culture to find acceptable
ways to integrate the affective into its understanding of human nature
created a deprivation filled in part by cultivating sentiment, and

especially in fostering the image of woman's melting sensibility. Rather than simply deploring such subterfuges deployed by women in response to patriarchal constraints, Poovey maintains that there *had* to be some psychological rewards—for women as well as for men—in order for the broad acceptance of traditional gender roles to be accepted by both sexes. She shows that the distortions of care are embedded in the structures of the patriarchal institutions.[9] It is no surprise, then, that Camilla distorts, even sacrifices, her affective mien as a caring person to carefulness—a watchful attention that characterizes the dominant ideology.

The puzzling contradictions that the affective scenes in the novel entail point to other cultural issues embedded in those of gender and ideology. One is that of the modern critic-reader's expectation of "sufficiency" in narratives of sensibility. A traditional view expects the novels to fulfill such narrative conventions as orderly development of plot and character, verisimilitude, and rational action, and dismisses any deviation from this norm. However, to excuse *Camilla*'s deviation from such criteria by citing patriarchal constraints upon female writers doesn't really question the narrative conventions themselves. In other words, affect-provoking scenes of female vicissitudes still carry the negative connotation attributed to female sensibility in a male-dominated culture. Our tradition has implicitly feminized the sentimental, episodic novel, regarding it as deviant from the architectonics of plot.

Nancy K. Miller argues against the unquestioned "plots and plausibilities" of literary practices by focusing on the fact that women have been excluded from both our concept of literature and the literary critical enterprise.[10] In other words, the principle of narrative sufficiency may not be the same for women as for men. Terry Eagleton adopts this position and asks whether or not "those who are stripped of power from the outset, excluded by the rules of discourse from full subjecthood, [can] enter the power game at all without being instantly falsified? And is it any less misinterpretable to stay silent?"[11]

Those institutional practices that constitute the literary are inherently political, for they determine not only our notion of how a text performs but also the "who" that performs it. Everything is at stake in which version of author, work, and critic we enact. Teresa de Lauretis summarizes the issue for those texts and critics marginalized by institutional practices as follows: "For what is finally at stake is not so much how 'to make visible the invisible' as how to produce the condition of visibility for a different social subject."[12] A closer look, then, at "the wilder wonders of the Heart" may provide some possibilities for which "a different social subject" need not remain a "fiction." And yet no theory of sensibility or its peculiar practice in a novel like *Camilla* is possible so long as the conceptual understanding of those exploring the affective remains the same as that of those they question. In *Camilla*, the dialectic of rationality-affectivity is held up for questioning.

This opposition between rationality and affectivity is more complicated than a gendered alignment: male/reason, female/feeling.[13] At stake here is not just the commonplace notion that "reason needs feeling and feeling needs reason"; rather the crucial issue is the eighteenth-century inheritance of Cartesian doubt that questions the truth-revealing character of our relationship with the world, and of religious doubt (Pascal's *logique du cœur*) that questions the truth-revealing character of belief.[14] If we begin to doubt our relationship to the world (which does *not* preclude error and illusion), then the truth of the "wilder wonders of the Heart"—whether the truth of instinct, impulse, modal attunement, conscience, or even for that matter, narratives of sensibility—can no longer bear meaning as truth. No longer a "truth bearer" for culture, affectivity itself becomes a fiction whose only truth-space lies within the work of fiction. Blind to an affectivity that is both feeling *and* reflective, Camilla assumes that her nature is *nothing but* feeling. In thinking so, Camilla exemplifies and therefore critiques a culture whose subject-centered model of reasoning excludes feeling, reifies both reason and feeling, and doubts our relationship to the world. She and Edgar graphically demonstrate how a skewed rationality that denies its affective grounding propels reasoning toward doubt.

II

The story is of an impulsive girl of modest means, niece of a doting and foolish rich uncle, who becomes engaged to a wealthy and proper gentleman named Edgar Mandlebert. Edgar is enchanted with Camilla's sweet spontaneity and "melting sensibility," but he insists punctiliously that she prove herself possessed of the virtues of a wife.

Camilla unwittingly obstructs the flow of Edgar's desire when she
ventures "into the world," incurs a small and secret debt, and falls
into ambiguous situations that convince him that she is a coquette
and a "trifler." Wounded by his "misconstructions," she breaks off
the engagement. Shortly thereafter, her father goes to prison for her
small debt. The final and crucial hundred pages describe the prodigal
heroine as standing condemned before the court of her own "all-
feelings" role as the abuser of those she loves, and as a contrite,
disordered outcast from the culture that "castes" her. Finally, she
is redeemed by her sufferings and rewarded for them with marriage.

Camilla's character is described as one that "called for more
attention to its developement than to its formation":

> Her qualities had a power which, without consciousness how, or
> consideration why, governed her whole family. The airy thought-
> lessness of her nature was a source of perpetual amusement; and
> if sometimes her vivacity raised a fear for her discretion, the
> innocence of her mind reassured them after every alarm. The
> interest which she excited served to render her the first object
> of the house. . . . Her spirits were volatile, but her heart was ten-
> der; her gaiety had a fascination; her persuasion was irresistible.
> (51–52)

From this description, Camilla exemplifies a particular ideal of femininity; those who praise her adhere to a common belief in those
volatile, gay, and tender virtues associated with the spontaneous
nature of the female. From this passage, it is clear that these virtues
are on the whole unreflective; in other words, "gaiety," "vivacity,"
and "volatile spirits" form the "innocence of her mind." In fact
Camilla's virtues, the novel says, "are *all* feelings." For this reason,
family and friends alike not only enjoy but also indulge the "airy
thoughtlessness of her nature." Thus, it is not the balanced judgment
of a rational Cecilia, but Camilla's airy thoughtlessness that has "a
power" which "governed her whole family."

A display of sentiment, then, is exactly what "served to render
her the first object of the house." Compounding the family indulgence
of Camilla is Edgar's attitude that avows, "What a heart . . . is here!
what feelings, what tenderness, what animation!—O, what a heart!"
(326). Encouraged to be unreflective, Camilla openly displays her

sentiments even as she egregiously conceals them from her own understanding.

It cannot be overemphasized that the social code that dictates Camilla's virtues as "all feelings" conditions the feminine role she unthinkingly assumes and later calculatingly adopts. It is no wonder, then, that Camilla's nature, "whose impulses have no restraints," together with Edgar's "serious and meditative disposition . . . observant of the errors of others" are, as Mrs. Arlbery says, calculated to make them wretched.

After Camilla is downcast over Edgar's seeming indifference, Mrs. Arlbery gives her that harshly realistic lecture. She outlines the way a female can realize her desires by taking advantage of the contradictory standard that demands *both* the reflective judgment to avoid impropriety and the artless behavior that abjures reflection. She is careful to enumerate the monetary considerations that can grant freedom and security after marriage and insists that a little jealousy in Edgar will help Camilla's cause. She also contends that the guilelessness of Camilla's character enables Edgar to ascertain her feelings for him and thereby take advantage of them. Edgar's calculations (as even *he* later admits) cause him "doubtfully to watch her every action and suspiciously to judge her every motive" (901).

Mrs. Arlbery, with her hardheaded practical wisdom has a great deal to say about Edgar's character, and analyzes why this "frozen" youth needs to be "worked up into a little sensibility." Just as his seeming lack of sensibility contrasts with Camilla's strength of feeling, so Edgar's "watching" is "calculated" to make the impulsive Camilla miserable:

> He is a watcher; and a watcher, restless and perturbed himself, infests all he pursues with uneasiness. He is without trust, and therefore without either courage or consistency. To-day he may be persuaded you will make his happiness; to-morrow [*sic*], he may fear you will give him nothing but misery. Yet it is not that he is jealous of any other; 'tis of the object of his choice he is jealous, lest she should not prove good enough to merit it. . . . I have an instinctive aversion to those cold, haughty, drawing-back characters, who are made up of the egotism of looking out for something that is wholly devoted to them. (482, 483)

Arlbery's comments reveal her understanding of the male-female relationship as a mutually determining opposition—one that she advises Camilla to exploit. Hence, her advice represents a view of gender as a play of power. Seeing she has gained a point, she urges Camilla to make Edgar jealous by encouraging Sir Sedley: "If there is any way . . . of animating him for a moment out of himself, it can only be by giving him a dread of some other" (483). This strategy will enable Camilla to display both her power and disinterest. Arlbery convincingly ends her peroration with this assessment of Edgar's character: "Mandlebert is a creature whose whole composition is a pile of accumulated punctilios. He will spend his life in refining away his own happiness" (484). She concludes that Edgar, enslaved to law, will not scruple to break a heart as long as his honor "cannot be arraigned of breaking any bond."

Mrs. Arlbery's keen argument cuts through Camilla's modest sentiments by appealing to her *reason* while answering to her *desires*: "A picture so flattering to all her best feelings, and dearest wishes" (484). Her whole being is fascinated with the idea of proving her disinterest to Edgar and exonerating herself. Burney assigns to this idea the "real name" of "coquetry": "a scheme which, if proposed to her [Camilla] under its real name . . . she would have fled and condemned." Camilla resists thinking upon Mrs. Arlbery's realistic appraisal of her situation in order to dwell "upon nothing . . . except the one dear and inviting project of proving disinterestedness" (484). Camilla cherishes a belief in the purity of her own motives, which prevents her from acknowledging the truth of Arlbery's assessment even as she pursues the latter's agenda of exploitation.

Edgar, in turn, wishes for a perfect female: ingenuously artless, absolutely trustworthy, and totally devoted to him. He is passionately enamored of Camilla's artless character (actually of his own preconception of the female essence "so beautiful in its total ignorance of every species of scheme, every sort of double measure, every idea of secret view and latent expedient"), and yet he fears that society will spoil her affections and ingenuousness (671). His mentor and counterpoint to Mrs. Arlbery, the learned and wise Dr. Marchmont, stringently advises him not to propose marriage until Camilla passes a period of "probation" and he has "positively ascertained her actual possession of those virtues with which she appears to be endowed" (159). The scrupulous doctor comments:

You must study her. . . . Whatever she does, you must ask yourself
this question: 'Should I like such behaviour in my wife?' Whatever
she says, you must make yourself the same demand. Nothing must
escape you; you must view as if you had never seen her before;
the interrogatory, *Were she mine?* must be present at every look,
every word, every motion . . . ; even justice is insufficient during
this period of probation. . . . To avoid all danger of repentance,
you must become positively distrustful. (159, 160)

Instead of inquiring, 'Is this right in her?' the mysogynist doctor
insists, "You must simply ask, 'Would it be pleasing to me?'" Scru-
tinizing the motives of "the whole sex," he further cautions that
every female imbibes the idea that "a good establishment must be
her first object in life" (161). Marchmont's warning, based on the
rational principles of the age, celebrates a method of empirical proof
that will assuage doubt by banishing uncertainty. Though his advice
is often mentioned by the critics as a prime example of patriarchal
abuse, there is as much irony in it as in Mrs. Arlbery's wisdom.
In fact, Marchmont himself later admits that his opinion is based
upon his own loss in love. The immediate effect, however, is as
deflating for Edgar as Arlbery's advice was for Camilla. Filled now
with "a distrust of himself . . . struck to the soul with the apprehension of failing to gain her affection, and wounded . . . his confidence
was gone; his elevation of sentiment was depressed; a general mist
clouded his prospects, and a suspensive discomfort inquieted his
mind" (161, 162). After soberly meditating upon this advice, Edgar
determines "to guard his views, till he could find some opportunity
of investigating" Camilla's feelings (163). His calculating and doubtful stance promotes a mistrust that precipitates his painful misconstructions and Camilla's errors, and eventually erodes their
relationship and dissolves their engagement.

The major male figures' demands in the form of Edgar's mistrust,
Sir Hugh's indiscriminate indulgence, and Mr. Tyrold's pietistic sympathy amount to an insistence that Camilla please them by being
pleased to serve their pleasure. Such a skewed understanding of a
woman's affectivity encourages Camilla to believe that thoughtlessness means an absence of thought. Only when circumstances absolutely demand it does Camilla reluctantly examine her own motives.
Because "she had wished to fly even from herself, rather than venture

to investigate feelings so unwelcome" (168), she seems deliberately to avoid the conscious exercise of her obvious intelligence:

> She did not ask herself why; she did not consider the uselessness of flying for one hour what she must encounter the next. The present moment was all she could weigh; and, to procrastinate any evil, seemed, to her ardent and active imagination, to conquer it. (154)

Again like Evelina, Camilla falls prey to behavior that encourages misunderstandings; but unlike Evelina and Cecilia, modesty no longer *signifies* female virtue, since for Camilla, "feelings *are* all virtues." Hence, within the social context of this novel, "virtue" is an affective immediacy; it lacks a past ("the present moment was all she could weigh"); it defers the future ("to procrastinate . . . seemed . . . to conquer"); it liberates immediate desire from any external threat or "evil." This impulsive spontaneity is implicitly touted over propriety based on prudent judgment or virtue based on human distinction. Consequently, Camilla finds an incentive to act against her best interests by acting according to impulses that "have no restraint." In addition, her utterly calculating stance of acting uncalculating provides her with *rational* reasons to reinforce her "ardent imagination." Not only do Camilla's family and Edgar laud her artlessness, but Mrs. Arlbery reasons with Camilla against an *un*reflective, therefore "artless" artlessness. It is only when Camilla's public displays of sensibility can be seen as rejecting the reason that forgets its origin in an affective attunement to the world that her reasoning can be understood.

Camilla bases her reasoning that abjures reason upon a patriarchal norm. Nearly halfway through the novel in a letter encompassing an entire chapter, Mr. Tyrold, having already surmised Camilla's love for Edgar, writes her a "sermon" delineating this norm. He acknowledges that the "temporal destiny of woman is enwrapt in still more impenetrable obscurity than that of man," and he admits that female education succeeds or fails in accordance with the humors and expectations of her husband (356, 357). Notwithstanding this "impenetrable destiny" of woman, however, he blithely outlines for Camilla its "laws."

Throughout this remarkable sermon, Mr. Tyrold expresses private doubts about the public norm he upholds, while also doubting the public practice of his privately held beliefs. For example, even though he believes in "equality of freedom" for women, he obviates its practice when assuming that female action is limited by boundaries "which custom forbids your sex to pass." These limits are: "an unreturned female regard" that signals "ungoverned passions," and, even if its origin is in artlessness, a lack of discretion that signals forwardness and welcomes censure (357, 358). For these reasons, he advises, Camilla must not reveal her preference for Edgar until after he first declares himself to her. Again Mr. Tyrold contradicts himself when reminding her that delicacy, "an attribute so peculiarly feminine," is an *inherent* female trait while also warning her that only "agitated" feelings could cause her to forget "its appropriate laws, its minute exactions, its sensitive refinements" (359–60). Because of the "uncertainty of the female fate," Tyrold implicitly admits to this contradiction when he justifies the way he has brought up Camilla "without any specific expectation." Accordingly, he determines to inculcate in her "simplicity," "docility," and "accommodation," implying that the best education for a woman is a flexible accommodation to the whims and whimsical laws of her husband.

The narrator summarizes the "radical defect" of Camilla's character as an "imagination that submitted to no control" (84). This definition admits that the female imagination cannot be controlled even by the "laws" that constitute her nature. In other words, Camilla's "radical defect" is paradoxically also the source of her fascination to others: it "proved not any antidote against her attractions" and even "possessed, by magnetic pervasion, the witchery to create sympathy in the most serious" (84). Tyrold reassures Camilla that "good sense" will convince her that it is not "strength of mind" which she wants but "reflection, to obtain a strict and unremitting control over your passions" (359, 361). Appropriately double-minded about such contradictory advice, Camilla responds by appearing to Edgar as both unworthy and unstable in her affection. Clearly the norm for female behavior and its attendant "laws" are as full of contradictions as the wilder wonders of the heart.

Absent from Tyrold's assessment and absent too from the wider implications of that conceptualized female standard is the understanding that what he most admires in Camilla is also what he

heartily disapproves—even though he admits that disquisition about
"the abstract truth" of a position is fruitless without "some proof
of its practicability." Accordingly, in spite of Camilla's wish to obey
her father's admonition, thereby proving her docile accommodation,
and in spite of her active efforts to implement his advice toward
Edgar, thereby proving her disinterest, her feelings and her thoughts
remain divided. She must appear interested in Edgar in order to
encourage his declaration, yet also disinterested in order to prevent
his disapprobation. This complexity of interest and disinterest must
be appropriately communicated to him, not by direct and plain
speech, not even by indirect speech, but solely by her silent behavior.
That is, she must be governed by the delicacy that is her peculiar
attribute as woman, be obedient to its laws, and at the same time
be entirely spontaneous. Mr. Tyrold's sermon still pays lip service
to the norm of female decorum expressed in the earlier novels, and
to "delicacy" as Camilla's innate feminine characteristic, but with
the important difference that her sensibility is no longer under the
absolute sway of that norm. That difference is the basis for Camilla's
belief in the boundlessness of her affectivity and is exemplified in
her hysterical behavior during the concluding crisis in the novel.

As noted earlier in Arlbery's advice and reiterated in the sermon,
Camilla must restrain any appearance of her preference in order to
avoid censure. Consequently, she seems predictably uncaring when
she follows her father's advice and does not attend to Edgar. Likewise,
she seems predictably uncaring when other men attend to her as
well, so that Edgar is sure she is "thus versed in the common
dissipation of coquetry" (461). And yet when Camilla follows Mrs.
Arlbery's advice, she becomes entangled with Sir Sedley and dis-
gusted with herself. As a result, when she turns to other suitors to
avoid Sir Sedley, she seems *to all* to be a "trifler." Finally, when her
association with Mrs. Berlinton makes her an object of general
attention, Edgar is certain "the degradation from the true female
character is already begun!" (444). To comport herself in a manner
associated with coquetry deceitfully exploits males, but to act coquettish and conceal it from herself equally exploits her personal
integrity; thus, Mrs. Arlbery says: "Your artlessness, your facility,
and your innocence, with his knowledge, nay, his very admiration
of them, will operate but to separate you" (455).

If Camilla understood (or even had an incentive to understand) "the perverseness of spirit which grafts desire on what is denied," she might be able to obviate the dialectic of female artlessness/female artifice. But in order for Camilla to acknowledge her own desire, she would also have to understand the need to deny it under a principle of innocence which necessarily excludes—at least overtly—any understanding of desire. Nonetheless, Camilla's desire is made conspicuous by its absence from her discourse; she lacks even a vocabulary in which to shape her desires. Within such a vacuum of understanding, trifling with male desire under the rubric of coquetry acknowledges a female's power but not her understanding of desire. Moreover, when doubting Camilla's trustworthiness, Edgar displays no more understanding of his own desire than she does, even as he pursues that which *he* denies. The dynamics of this interplay of desire are highly opaque.

If Burney's description of desire as that which is grafted upon what is denied were translated into modern terms, it would come very close to Lacan's description of the process of desire.[15] According to Jane Gallop, male desire is linked to fear and therefore tied to the future as an imminent threat, while female desire is viewed as loss in the past and hence takes the form of nostalgia.[16] Edgar's fear and Camilla's nostalgia are respectively forms of mistrust or doubt, and sentiment, for "man is threatened with loss, woman is deprived." "What Lacan calls desire," Gallop says, is "a desire constitutively unsatisfied and unsatisfiable because its 'object' simply cannot ever be defined."[17] Thus desire objectified is always alienating. Only if Edgar and Camilla learn to negotiate with desire as a principle that always, elsewhere grafts onto what it denies can they recognize the Other's desire and accommodate it. That is, the affectivity and reasoning that they displace could be assimilated only if they understood the mutual determination of those displacements. The wisdom of the age available to them in Arlbery and Marchmont's advice and Tyrold's sermon is not adequate for such an understanding. What is open to scrutiny in this context of desire is the fantasy that objectivity can be uncontaminated by desire and that affectivity can be distinct from rationality. In spite of Camilla's puzzling behavior and Edgar's doubts—or perhaps because of them—Edgar proposes to her. The period of their engagement should abrogate all doubts

between them, but Edgar and Camilla are too mistaken about one
another and too lacking in self-understanding to reach that point.

Burney's extraordinary understanding of the interplay of desire
serves to highlight Edgar and Camilla's misunderstanding of each
other. It appears to Edgar that Camilla is still merely trifling with
him. He moans to Dr. Marchmont in a "paroxysm of sudden misery
and torturing jealousy": "Explain, expound to me this work of
darkness and amazement; tell me why, with every appearance of
the most artless openness, I find her thus eternally disingenuous and
unintelligible?" (571). For her part, Camilla finds Edgar cold and
rational and, hurt by his behavior, vows that "she would not risk
another mark of his cold superiority, but restore to him his liberty
and leave him master of himself" (582). At this juncture, Camilla
reveals that she does understand the adversarial role of gender when
Edgar appears before her dejected and "she read in it her power"
(585).

Encouraged, Camilla follows Mrs. Arlbery's advice: "In the present disordered state of the opinions of Edgar, the only way . . . was
to alarm his security, by asserting her own independence." But, like
Evelina, she also allows herself to be directed by lowbred characters
into questionable compromises: "Accident, want of due consideration, and sudden recollection . . . of the worldly doctrine of Mrs.
Arlbery, had led Camilla, once more, into the semblance of a character, which, without thinking of, she was acting. Born simple and
ingenuous . . . an untoward contrariety of circumstances, playing
upon feelings too potent for deliberations, had eluded her into a
conduct as mischievous in its effects and as wide from artlessness in
its appearance" (679). Camilla calculates, but does not necessarily
reflect upon, the semblance of a character so "wide from artlessness,"
perhaps justifying those who see her disordered conduct as "whimsical reasoning."

Beneath the dialectical opposition of those who condemn and those
who excuse Camilla's version of sensibility lies the sedimentation of
a whole intellectualist culture. This tradition still relegates the spontaneous to some sort of impulsive lack of foresight or absence of
rational thought rather than sees it as an integral part of thought
not available to individual self-consciousness. Camilla is encouraged
to *be* spontaneous premeditatively, at the very least a contradiction
in terms. Her problem arises from using calculation to convince

herself of her artlessness. Spontaneity does not imply, as she assumes, acting whimsically or even unrationally, nor does it imply being consciously aware of how artless she appears to others.

Inasmuch as Camilla exemplifies a "melting sensibility" normally identified with the feminine, she also demonstrates the lack of thought associated with impulse. However, the spontaneous act that constitutes—at least provisionally—the subject is not a fixed point of departure, but an ongoing interaction with the world, a fusing of possibilities, the horizon of the human with the horizon of a world.[18] Spontaneity arises from within a practiced engagement of the human with the world—from within a habitude of past possibilities that enable fruitful improvisation in the moment. It is not some externally contrived norm for "artlessness" that an individual consciously adopts.

Camilla thinks herself incapable of forming a coherent plan of action in her strenuous efforts to maintain her spontaneity and preserve her artlessness. Her mother assesses Camilla's behavior by saying that "were her understanding less good, I should less heavily weigh her errours [*sic*]; but she sets it apart, to abandon herself to her feelings. Alas! poor thing! they will now themselves be her punishers" (862). Her mother assumes that Camilla willfully sets aside thought *and* willfully (i.e., deliberately) abandons herself to feeling. Within such a cultural fragmentation of thought and feeling, Camilla assiduously avoids the detached reflective posture of the rational and chooses instead, sometimes by not choosing at all, to yield, as in the case of Indiana's charge that she cares for Edgar, to the exigencies of the immediate. Camilla's only thought is that of satisfying herself of "the innocence of her intentions." She assumes that one's intentions are fully available to consciousness. Further, she assumes, like Rousseau, that sincerity answers for and can excuse past actions. Since she doesn't know "what alteration she could make in her behaviour," she concludes, after rejecting various plans, that "to make none would best manifest her freedom from self-reproach" (169). For Camilla, "to avert immediate evil was ever resistless to her ardent mind" (743).

To understand either Edgar's "disordered state" or Camilla's "ardent mind" one must disentangle the reciprocity of their needs, and see each as a function of the other. Edgar's wish to prohibit anything not available to his control makes him the quintessential

intellectualist and an acute doubter. Driven by his own unacknowledged and unruly affectivity, which threatens the orderliness of his
world, his demand for certitude and control expresses itself in requiring perfection from Camilla.

If Edgar erroneously thinks of himself as the detached observer,
she thinks of herself as the selfless servant, concerned only with
pleasing him. Like Evelina, Camilla assumes her motives, "what in
her was designed with innocence," to be pure, untainted by self-
interest (681). The very fact that she "designs" her innocence and
conceals from herself her desire serves to shake both her judgment
and sensibility:

> The ardour of her imagination, acted upon by every passing idea,
> shook her Judgment from its yet unsteady seat, and left her at
> the mercy of wayward Sensibility—that most delicate, but irreg-
> ular power, which now impels to all that is most disinterested for
> others, now forgets all mankind, to watch the pulsations of its
> own fancies. (680)

Burney's definition of sensibility *clearly* distinguishes between an
affectivity directed away from the self and toward others ("impels
to all that is most disinterested for others") and an affectivity that
watches, as Camilla's does, "the pulsations of its own fancies." Her
self-absorption closely parallels the earlier description of Edgar's
doubtful rumination that also watches "the pulsations of its own
fancies."

Edgar's refusal to admit his own affective bond to the world
absolutizes the impulsive Camilla into an object of the very sensibility
that he has repressed. This kind of objectivity works in much the
same way as Descartes describes in his *Meditations*—it dissolves the
concrete in the mood (meditations) of doubt which clouds everything
that is subjective with an aura of objectivity.[19] It is precisely Edgar's
own passion to possess her affection exclusively that drives him
relentlessly to watch her even as his passion reveals to us his forgotten
sensibility. In taking measure of Camilla, he is so emotionally entangled in the field of his own measurement (judging her worthy
and true to a standard he assumes to be universal) that it is impossible
for him to separate her as object from his calculating stance. Accordingly, his empirical truth-claims reflect the ethos of his own

conceptual framework. This ethos is not the reflective posture of genuine questioning but the debilitating and ultimately negating stance of doubt which:

> In its most harmless form . . . permeates English empiricism, where the meaningfulness of the sensibly given is dissolved into data of sense perception. . . . Empiricism is only seemingly a vindication of the sense; actually it rests on the assumption that only common-sense arguing can give them meaning, and it always starts with a declaration of non-confidence in truth- or reality-revealing capacity of the senses.[20]

This description of empirical doubt parallels what Burney calls "Suspicion" and the "acquired distrust of experience."

Although Edgar may appear to Camilla as cold, proud, and rational, we know from the text that he is adrift in a tide of moods and feelings. Furthermore, Dr. Marchmont has taught him expressly to resist seeing the affective as an integral part of reason, implicitly therefore to miss seeing that his displaced affectivity has been projected onto the female sex: "There is commonly so little stability, so little internal hold, in the female character," says the doctor (654). For them, the female is both essence, all feeling, and nonessence, unstable, uncertain, uncontrollable. Thus, both Edgar and Dr. Marchmont can only conclude that Camilla is "a confirmed coquette" and suspect her every move.

We have learned so far that the role Camilla unthinkingly adopts constricts her understanding when she plays to male desire in its reified form. She forces herself to appear as the object-woman, which "he" has already objectified. For Edgar, fearing change, ultimately fearing Camilla herself, means fearing the impulses he can't rationally, consciously control. He thinks that affects need the absolute restraint that rationality alone can provide, while she thinks the affects need an absolute freedom that only her premeditated artlessness can assure. If Camilla as Edgar's displaced affectivity seems subject only to the play of mood, emotion, and caprice, in short to the incertitude of change, then his desire to control her wishfully circumvents affectivity itself and its discontinuity. Edgar's attitude causes him to become a voyeur of Camilla by attributing to her an essence, an invented and hidden reality to penetrate and control, certain that her innocence hides mystery, that her ingenuousness covers duplicity: "Can it be Camilla, the ingenuous, the artless Camilla, I find it so difficult to fathom, to comprehend, to trust?" (481). Edgar's standard of the rational requires rule over the affectivity that enchants as it worries him. By giving himself over to his love for her, to a chaos of sensibility, he sees himself as bound by Camilla's power: "Why, though I have cast myself wholly into her power, she retains all her mystery . . . she heightens it into deceit next perjury?" (571).

Since decorum forbids female initiative and Edgar at this point in the narrative seldom listens but to condemn her, Camilla never finds an opportunity to explain herself adequately. Edgar is predisposed "doubtfully to watch her every action, and suspiciously to judge her every motive" (901). That "school of suspicion" which Edgar belongs to is Cartesian. Descartes became convinced that man in his search for truth and knowledge could no longer trust either his senses or his reason.[21] Similarly, Edgar doubts himself, doubts Camilla, doubts his observations of her, and yet "wished to obtain from her immediately the unlimited trust, which immediately, and for ever, he meant to repose in her" (554). With the legacy of Cartesian suspicion behind him, Edgar seeks from Camilla the answers that will always reflect the doubt with which he began.

Camilla's alternative to Edgar's mistrust is to make herself into an object: a self-concerned narcissist who cultivates her artifice. This artifice ensures that Camilla identify with the image of herself that Edgar holds up to her. In her description of Camilla, Burney foreshadows an issue that only gradually comes to clarity in recent discussions, where, for example, Derrida makes explicit Nietzsche's extraordinary understanding of the image of narcissism and woman. Derrida talks about the doubled image (artless and artful) of "woman" as follows: "Either, at times, woman is woman because she gives, *because she gives* herself, while the man for his part takes, possesses, indeed takes possession. Or else, at other times, she is woman because, in giving, she is in fact *giving herself for*, is simulating, and consequently assuring the possessive mastery for her own self."[22] As a creature of artifice, "she" cannot be fooled into believing as "he" does that she has some essence or core identity. What she doesn't see as artifice as well, however, is the illusion inherent in that essentialist idea of personhood. In other words, Camilla assumes that she *is* "Woman" only insofar as she gives herself over to Edgar and accommodates her desires to his. When she gives herself according to Edgar's expectation, then she is the essence of woman. But when she plays the coquette, even unwittingly, she dissembles and mystifies herself into an object that *seems* to divide her. As an object, however, she retains her control over Edgar's desire by rejecting his possession of her; thus she is "Woman" again—in the sense of those human impulses that cannot be controlled. Nietzsche, Derrida, and Lacan analyze what Burney long ago articulated and historically situated in her novel—"that amazing assemblage of all possible contrarieties, in which one thing alone is steady—the perverseness of spirit which grafts desire on what is denied."

The doubled "Woman" that Camilla represents in this novel is a myth that remakes itself as the true; she receives instruction about woman's essential frailty: an image of woman which she, by deferring (or appearing to defer) to it, verifies. On her part "fixed in her mind, like 'truths from holy writ'" is an image of Edgar as that of "inalienable steadiness, unalterable honour"—an image that cannot account for his affective unsteadiness. Camilla "checked every idea that did not represent Edgar as unstable and consistent," and believed him "insensible and hard of heart" (541). When physically absent from her, Edgar is present as a kind of watchful voice of authority, a standard of correctness against which she measures herself. On the one hand, he is sure that he knows the "true feminine character," while on the other, "not knowing who or what she was, [he] simply filled up the doubts in his own mind, by the bias of his own character" (659). Likewise, Camilla's surrender to sensibility refigures herself as his enemy, his repressed, unacknowledged affectivity. Her affectivity disrupts order and elides the boundaries of gender, custom, and identity.

The purported desire to spare the female the pain of "reality" and keep her artless—"How far more highly is the true feminine character preserved, where surmise is not raised, than where it can be parried!" (476)—masks an inherent opposition of male to female, an assumption that the female is absolutely other and not responsible for herself. By contrast, female manipulation of the male is the mirror image of this activity. Her difference from him is threatening to one who sees herself as thoughtless and therefore powerless; yet, paradoxically, she brings him under control by her own self-deceit and subterfuge. Camilla "knew, with certainty incontrovertible, that his fate was at her disposal, from the instant he acknowledged openly her power over his feelings" (544). She knows without doubt that he is in her power when he reveals the feelings he is wont to deny. Likewise, the male attributes power to the "helpless" female. Edgar says of the alluring Mrs. Berlinton: "There is surely much to fear from her early possession of power" (475). Consequently, both aim at a total and exclusive mastery over the other; both simultaneously reject and desire their opposites; hence, both become for each other the measure of desire. Since this desire is always "grafted" elsewhere, it will, for them, inevitably be frustrated where it is denied.

III

Frustrated desire bespeaks the pathos of a cultural gap, a lack of options for saying and thus understanding who one is. Representational explanations of who Camilla is abound despite a growing lack of correspondence between the explanations and her presentation of herself. Others simply assume that she cannot speak in her own voice and cannot articulate her desires, that she needs someone else with authority to speak for her. Because she is made voiceless, both by her "too passive facility" and by her silence, others feel a duty to speak for her. Edgar is "charmed with the candour of her silence." She often seeks his just and timely advice, derived from the strength of his reflective powers and the unassailable assurance of his convictions. Nevertheless, he is highly displeased when Camilla fails to accept his proffered advice; like others in the novel, he is convinced that he has the whole truth about who she is—except that "who" remains a mystery to him and a capricious subject to us.

When a series of crises demand that Camilla think about her own thinking, when the act of concealment gnaws at her—she has kept her debt a secret and employed a usurer—its practice seems "more dreadful to bear than the loss even of Edgar himself," because "the latter blackened every prospect of felicity; but the former . . . seemed to strike even at her innocence" (757). Preserving what she believes to be her achieved and constant artlessness is *more* important to her than *even* the loss of Edgar. Like Evelina, she traps herself into accepting a prevailing belief in a static female identity that essentially turns her into a product. Like Cecilia, she feels assaulted by the

very affectivity that assigns to her its safekeeping. Camilla's dis-
avowal of the rational limits her thought, prohibits her access to
representational language, and amidst several scenes of great drama,
produces her "hysteria."

Camilla's emotional crisis in the final one hundred pages of the
novel is variable and extreme even for one who is "all feeling," and
until recently, little critical reflection has been given to this climactic
episode. She screams rather than laments, cries rather than weeps;
she flies about frantically or falls down in prostration; she shakes,
shrieks, wrings her hands, shivers, moans, raves. The sustained
violence of Camilla's sensibility is a stumbling block that can puzzle
the reader. Neither events nor feelings leading up to Camilla's crisis
adequately prepare the reader for the extremity of her response. It
seems astonishing that her crime, if it be a crime, is merely accumulating a modest debt, due mainly to her ignorance, benevolence,
and trust in the wrong persons. The cultural norms she so unthinkingly adopts cannot answer for her despair nor explain her hysteria
nigh unto madness.

Learning that her beloved father, Mr. Tyrold, must go to Win-
chester Prison because of her debt, "words of alarming incoherency
proclaimed the danger menacing her intellects, while agonies nearly
convulsive distorted her features, and writhed her form" (824). Serious reflection or explanation seems impossible for her, and she
"could not write: to kneel, to weep, to sue, was all she could bear
to plan" (828). Beside herself from "feelings overstrained, and nerves
dreadfully shattered," she wishes "to sink to death." Camilla's reflections, even when thinking about her once-betrothed, are a series
of self-condemnatory outpourings: "'Ah Edgar! . . . had I trusted you
as I ought . . . what misery had I been saved!—from this connexion—
from my debts—from every wide-spreading mischief!—I could then
have erred no more, for I should have thought but of your approv-
ance!'" (847, 848). After rushing precipitously all around the coun-
tryside and imagining herself abandoned by her family, she is nearly
delirious from fever and despair. She pens a dramatic and final
deathbed letter to her parents and another to Edgar.[23]

Camilla's letter to Edgar bears careful scrutiny as a final emotive
appeal to and assault upon his "frozen sensibility." Bearing the
superscription, "*Not to be delivered till I am dead,*" the letter is a voice
"in sufferance" for Camilla, since a direct expression of herself is

within her intellectual *power* but not within her cultural *right*. For
this reason, Camilla asks herself "shall I not . . . and may I not at
such a period [i.e., death], with innocence, with propriety, write
one poor word to him?" (870). The letter is an attempt to heal the
fractured rational and affective bond between Edgar and Camilla
and to overcome—as in the case of Evelina—cultural prohibition,
spatial separation, and conceptual distance. Illness prevents Camilla
from writing more than the following: "O Edgar! in this last farewell
be all displeasure forgotten!—from the first to the final moment of
my short life, dear and sole possessor of my heart!" (870). The
narrative voice explains that "the wish of death is commonly but
disgust of life, and looks forward to nothing further than release
from worldly care:—but the something yet beyond . . . the something
unknown, untried . . . now abruptly presented itself to her consideration" (872).

The "something unknown, untried" announces the death of
Camilla's calculations and past configuration. Confronted with her
own death, she has no future in view and for the first time thinks
about her thinking: she arrives at a conditional understanding of
her own emotional posturing in a dialogue with her conscience: "A
mist was cleared away that hitherto, obscuring every duty by de-
spondence, had hidden from her own perceptions the faulty basis of
her desire . . . that had concealed from her view the cruelty of this
[her] egotism" (872). The faulty basis of her desire lies in her "way-
ward Sensibility" that turns away from her relationship to the world
and turns toward the egotism of introspection. Living in a shell of
protective generalities, Camilla discovers herself to be inwardly
graceless.

She feels a "speechless apprehension" at the truth of this self-
revelation, and in her feverish delirium hears "a voice from within,
over which she thought she had no controul [*sic*], though it seemed
issuing from her vitals." The voice orders her to "write with thy
own hand thy claims, thy merits to mercy!" (875). "O, no! no! no!"
she protests, "let me not sign my own miserable insufficiency!"
Despite her objection, she is involuntarily forced to grasp "a pen of
iron" and write in "guilty characters." "These are thy deserts,"
sounds a voice; "write now thy claims." Once again, "unlicensed
by her will, her hand seized the iron instrument. . . . She wrote with
difficulty . . . but saw that her pen made no mark! She looked upon

the page, when she thought she had finished, . . . but the paper was blank!" (875, 876; ellipses in text).

Like a blank page, Camilla is without "claims," that is, without the right to speak for herself. She has no authority except that of the unnamed voice to "author" her own life, her own discourse, which in "issuing from her vitals," as a *logique du cœur,* leaves no marks. Unlike Evelina, Camilla cannot write reflexively because the patriarchal narrative voice, not Camilla herself, speaks for her in the already articulated lexicon of representation. She is still trapped within the discourse of authority that represents her to us and re-establishes the same conceptual barrier that she earlier tried to over-come by affectivity.

Since Camilla can only write her letter from "beyond the grave," in other words, beyond the representational barriers, Burney must use the narrative voice to enable Edgar to "hear" Camilla *before* she dies. The result is a deus ex machina, a wholly improbable and coincidental circumstance wherein Edgar appears at the same inn, agrees to read prayers to an unnamed "Lady who had gone out of her mind," and discovers the pledged locket he had given Camilla. The shock of Camilla's imminent death divests him of his previous doubt and mistrust and releases his suppressed feelings. Overcome with emotion at the sight of her, Edgar abandons his affective distance and writes a letter begging her remembrance of "our intuitive at-tachment" (879). Although she is too ill to read the letter, Camilla revives when a tear from Edgar's eye drops upon her "feeble" hand as a "testimony of his sensibility." She recovers when she sees Edgar "penetrated to anguish by her situation, [and] awakened to the tenderest recollections" (878). At long last, Edgar's "frozen sensi-bility" is thawed.

Camilla is restored to her family, all misunderstandings are cleared, and all that remains is for the lovers to reconcile formally. But once again, Camilla cannot declare her feelings for Edgar, so that this time Burney must contrive an eavesdropping scene where Edgar, concealed in the next room, hears Camilla plaintively explain to her father why they parted:

Accident . . . deluding appearances . . . and false internal reasoning on my part,—and on his, continual misconstruction! . . . I had ever the semblance, by some cruel circumstance, some inexplicable fatality of incident, to neglect his counsel, oppose his judgment, deceive his expectations, and trifle with his regard! (896)

The dialectic of feeling-reason reveals itself as "false reasoning" on her part and "continual misconstruction" on his.

By secretly listening to the private conversation, Edgar "hears" Camilla at last in the sense of openly attending to her, hears her through, as it were, the conceptual wall between them. However, as long as Edgar "overhears" Camilla, that is, hears her without being addressed by her, she says (shows) nothing *to* him. Whatever he overhears, whatever he believes for having overheard, is necessarily false. He rushes in upon the "drooping, shrinking, half expiring Camilla" after her admission, and bewails his "execrated doubt" in the face of "the sense that now breaks in" upon him that Camilla loves him (896). He is now willing to relinquish his Cartesian doubt on the basis of the "proof" that can be heard through a wall. Nonetheless, he is still at this point the objective observer standing outside the field of his own awareness, separating himself from his intimate bonds to it.

Camilla's rejection of the intellectual rigor of thinking and Edgar's rejection of his own affectivity raise an issue that was to have great significance in our day in the current debate over representation. Martin Heidegger grappled with the issue of value positing as *the* problem of the Enlightenment man. Edgar, as this doubter, retrieves his own forgotten affectivity by objectifying Camilla as absolute affectivity. Edgar wishes to compel Camilla's present to be permanent, to keep her untarnished from the world by devaluing her in positing her as a receptacle of value. To make her into an object disrupts her integrity as a provisional subject (not properly a subject at all) and obscures her as female, mystifying her into an object (not properly an object). Edgar can only validate her by forcing her to conform to his positing of her. This value positing activity, a form of subjectivism, is what Heidegger sees as the heart of the empirical demand for proof: "What a thing is in its Being is not exhausted by its being an object, particularly when objectivity takes the form of value. Every valuing, even where it values positively, is a subjectivizing. It does not let beings: be. Rather, valuing lets beings: be valid—solely as the objects of its doing."[24]

By validating her according to his dogmatic notion of female virtue Edgar makes himself a victim of his own passion. Thus, he is the Cartesian man who denies passion and fears its lack because he cannot discover his desire under the *structure* of reason, and because he cannot validate his affectivity under the *stricture* of reason. His rationality depends upon his prerational beliefs. Having to rely on "unprovable" belief causes him to fear the collapse of his "essential" being.

Camilla, on her side, sacrifices the self-discovery of reflexive thought; she lets a "self," that is, a "what" be determined for her rather than letting "who" be. Her rejection of reason reveals a thinking that refuses to think: "She had not seen her conduct in this light: yet her understanding refused to deny it might bear this interpretation" (476). To paraphrase Heidegger, because she is speaking against rationality and for affectivity, it is as though Camilla renounces the reign of thinking for that of arbitrary feelings, and thus, irrationalism proclaims the true ("Letter," 225). While the "pen of iron" is a current metonym for patriarchal authority (the privileging of the author), it is, nevertheless the only conceptual apparatus available to Camilla. However instinctively right her feelings may be, she is forever frustrated when only representational thought has a right to speak for her and mark her a "blank." Heidegger writes: "Occasionally we still have the feeling that . . . people disavow thought instead of taking pains to make it more thoughtful" ("Letter," 155). For this reason, when Camilla displays hysterical behavior and "sets aside understanding to abandon herself to her feelings," she chooses to disavow thought rather than become more thoughtful. Unable to explain herself—"I cannot continue silent, yet to whom may I address myself?"—her misery "exceeded all measure of restraint" (845, 827). She has the overwhelming feeling in the face of abstract rationality that a violence has been perpetrated against her by depriving her of "the power of thinking" (819). Because she cannot but accede to the division between emotion and reason Camilla cannot understand that intuition and impulse are already included in the activity of thought. That is, mood and feeling are not a separate state but an indivisible aspect of thinking.

Since Camilla's world is limited to meanings already given, to the categories of her language, she does not have a conceptual vocabulary with which she can adequately describe herself; decorum forbids her to give Edgar reasons for her behavior unless he first gives her his commitment and his leave to do so. Representative language itself, based on the narrowed view of the rational described in the discussion of *Cecilia,* does not sanction Camilla's use of the rational for explanations. Because representation delineates the rational and irrational according to gendered divisions when it dislocates reason from sensibility, Camilla must, like Cecilia, transmit an image of herself in the only form in which she can be understood: through the "blank" of her feelings. Where Cecilia believes that reason stands in the place of her desire, Camilla believes that affectivity stands in the place of her reason; she hides her desires and the larger significance of her feelings from her understanding. Where Cecilia can find no feelings that satisfy the rigor of her thought, Camilla finds ample reasons that confirm her own thoughtlessness. Where Cecilia exposes every thought and feeling to the scrutiny of the rational, Camilla excludes the rational from all sense of sensibility, thereby rationalizing her own calculation.

Camilla rejects a narratable past—recall her wish to avoid anything not answering to her desires—in order to accede to the immediate. To lose the world in this way makes the individual life unnarratable and ensures that Camilla will be present to others only by means of her distorted affectivity. If language is conceived as a thing among other things in the world, where does one whose "feelings are all virtues" find semantic space for herself within the prevailing commonsense view of language as object designator? The only space for her is outside the rational. In other terms, she finds her place in opposition to the rational: the affective as unnameable. Camilla laments this reductive (male) understanding of language when she says to her sister Lavinia:

> They are not like us, Lavinia. They think themselves free, if they have made no verbal profession; though they have pledged themselves by looks, by actions, by attentions, and by manners, a thousand, and a thousand times! (538)

She knows that one interprets the world "by looks, by actions, by attentions, and by manners," as well as by speech. This way of interpreting the world can only be understood when one is fully attuned to the world in an inseparable affective and rational bond.

In an attempt to compensate for thought reduced to the representable, Camilla privileges feeling over reason, and even over the norms of coherent speech: "As she could not in this instance declare what were her feelings, [she] remained mute and confounded" (342). She objectifies herself as the enabling condition of her resistance to reason and measures herself by her difference from Edgar. And again, denied the right to speech, she finds herself "deprived of the power of utterance, and looked a picture of speechless dismay" (825). In this instance, she does not use her sensibility to assault conceptual thought directly as rationality assails feeling, but indirectly attempts to bring near what abstract rationality has distanced, that is, the prereflective, affective attunement that permeates all thinking. Her sentiment presses feeling upon her, overwhelming her with its pathos in an effort to overcome what the rational keeps at a distance. This is one reason why *Camilla* abounds with pathos-evoking scenes.

The feelings of both Edgar and Camilla show us that feeling makes us receptive, that is, attunes us to the world in differing ways. "World" in this sense is a field of relations that reveals a "who," not a container of things holding a "what." As Josef Pieper claims, to have a world, to be related to the totality of existence can only belong to a being who is not a *what* but a *who*.[25] The form of knowing peculiar to Edgar, his conception of cognition, introduces a way of relating to the world from which woman and feeling are barred. Likewise, Camilla's form of taking account of the world resists the logical. Her display of sentiment is an attempt to make space for what is absent from discourse. Consequently, both ways of relating to the world tend to be reductionist, diminishing the possibilities available to the human. Her inexpressibility also exemplifies the narrowing of language where word is reduced to the abstract, denotative, and nominal. The terror she feels at the loss of speech, the loss of human bonds of communication, at the same time pays tribute to the importance of communal understanding, for language in this sense is both the reciprocal and revelatory creation of meaning. In other words language speaks and abides in the presence of this inseparable affective and rational relation to the world. By abandoning herself to sensibility, Camilla claims her only right to speak, an emotional outcry that also bespeaks her suffering. Nevertheless, the world that hears her grief still has no means of interpreting her cry because that cry has no "name." A world of objects nominalized

can find nothing "nameable" about Camilla's hysteria. Worse still,
affectivity itself becomes unnarratable and thus remains a "fiction."

To the last, Camilla resists taking responsibility for the shape of
her own destiny. This responsibility is a reflexive position: Camilla
would need to surrender an assumption about her essential being
as one who is *all* feeling in order to stand apart and re-think herself.
And she has shown that she refuses to take that risk when she shrinks
from the responsibility of the constraining "pen of iron"—a pen
that could give her a conditional name. Since she is given to understanding herself as lacking thought, she rejects rigor of thinking
when she rejects the form of rationality that leaves her affective
"mark" a "blank."

To the last, Camilla resists surrendering her artifice of artlessness.
That is, she will not consider herself as even a provisional being;
she would rather cling to herself as a "thing." Because she still sees
herself as a passive victim of misfortune, of "some cruel circumstance, some inexplicable fatality of incident"; and because she en-
visions herself according to an order arranged elsewhere (the
perspective of his gaze: "his judgment, his expectations, his regard"), she will sacrifice her language and speech in order to let
others say *what* she is. She will resist taking the pen of iron into her
conceptual grasp and making—and that means re-making—it her
own, so that it and her name are forever changed. The pen in the
hands of woman need not be that iron rod of the patriarchal author.
She still acquiesces to the role of the uncomprehending female: "This
is such a dream . . . so incredible . . . so unintelligible . . . I find it
entirely . . . impossible . . . impossible to comprehend any thing I see
or hear!" She still rejects herself as a person capable of thought: "If
I could understand in the least, what this all means . . . what—"
(897; ellipses in text). And she still expects patriarchal authority to
supply the meaning. She remains "disinherited" from the making
of meaning, from the right to speak for herself, as in the beginning
of the narrative when her name was excluded from her uncle's will.
The narrative ends, all the knots in their relationship untangled,
with Camilla's surrendering her thinking to Edgar, who as her husband "by generous confidence, became the repository of her *every*
thought."

As in the earlier two novels, Burney's narrative presents marriage
as the only narrative that can tell the *logique du cœur*. As more than

a stereotypical form of closure, marriage brings with it the guardianship of authority under which a female can speak, not only to her husband, but to her world. Only from there can her world become a field of relationships where she and her environment are one. Marriage is here a feeble attempt to repair the human, fragmented into gender, dissociated from feeling; but because marriage is also an extrinsically contrived union of duality, it cannot integrate reason and feeling reified as psychological states. Accordingly, the obligatory wedding is, to use Eagleton's words, "a consoling myth": an attempt to compensate for the displaced "name" and "fiction" of affectivity.

Burney carries these same issues over into *The Wanderer* where the as yet unresolved problem is woman's voice. Her silence, namelessness, and the way her name is tied to a radical understanding of language is not, as in the first three novels, obscured by the events outlined in the plot and the development of the heroine's character. In Burney's last novel, naming woman the "Wanderer," even naming itself *is* the emplotting event; and woman herself, as the margin of social discourse, becomes the precondition of narrative itself.

4

The Wanderer:
Naming Woman

All sorrows can be borne if you put them into a story or tell a story about them.

—Isak Dinesen

WHEN FANNY BURNEY DESCRIBES the protagonist in her last novel, *The Wanderer,* as "unknown, unnamed, without any sort of recommendation," she repeats the words she applied to herself as a writer, to her heroines as females, and to her condition as a woman.[1] The "unknown, unnamed" became a lifelong philosophical concern that found concrete expression in her voluminous writings, from her earliest diary addressed to "a certain Miss Nobody," to the authoring of her first novel, *Evelina,* by an author "without name, without recommendation, and unknown." Even in her last work, *Memoirs of Dr. Burney,* published in 1832 at the age of eighty, she remembers that as a writer she was "unpatronized, unaided, unknown." "Unknown, unnamed" became an inscription for all those female "scribblers" who took up the pen in an attempt to name their own narrative destinies.

In the eighteenth century, the ability to name and to author comes under the sway of representation, the model of philosophical thinking which represents human nature as a fixed concept, dictates the range of who and what is sayable, that is, nameable and socially acceptable. Under representation, women appear nameless not only in the traditional sense that they are named only by taking their husband's name, but also in that they have no authority to confer names, to employ the concept-invoking process that claims mastery over language. It is others who name them and so name their being and thereby conceal their be-ing.

Burney's novels reveal that in the dominant, Western system of meaning, women have no place *except* as Woman, the concept. An abstraction from a class of individuals (e.g., a common property), the concept is like a patriarchal surname that designates a familial relationship. The surname bears in common an inheritance which imposes (sur) above and (sur) over an individual a common term, and, in the case of patriarchy, unites those who confer names. One conceptual strategy for conferring identity and excluding difference is gender.

The *Wanderer* more clearly than Burney's earlier works thematizes the nameless as feminine and explores in a phenomenology of female difficulties the theory of representation that constitutes Woman as a concept. Luce Irigaray links concept and surname when she describes how women have been enmeshed in a highly conceptual system of naming.[2] The unnamed doesn't merely lack speech, it remains undisclosable, hidden by the concept that produces the condition of women's hysteria. Irigaray asks, "Does the hysteric speak? Isn't hysteria a privileged place for preserving—but 'in latency,' 'in sufferance'—that which does not speak? . . . Those aspects . . . that find themselves reduced to silence in terms of a culture that does not allow them to be expressed" (*TSNO*, 136). In other words, the properties of woman, the proper woman, and woman as property are all versions of the feminine conceptualized by representation in a patriarchal culture.[3]

Yet the uniquely human is emphatically not a collection of properties that make up the "what" of a person, so that when asked in an interview, "What is a woman," Irigaray replied, "The question 'what is . . . ? is the question—the metaphysical question—to which the feminine does not allow itself to submit." The questioner, in effect rewording the same question, then asked Irigaray for an alternative "concept" of femininity. She responded instead with another question:

Can anyone, can I, elaborate another, a different, concept of femininity? . . . To claim that the feminine can be expressed in . . . a concept is to allow oneself to be caught up again in a system of 'masculine' representations, in which women are trapped in a system of meaning. . . . In a woman('s) language, the concept as such would have no place. (*TSNO,* 122, 123)

In Burney's writings, women are caught up in that system of masculine representations and depicted as having no place except as a concept. Under representation the female seldom speaks, is often silenced. What Burney's other heroines, Evelina, Camilla, and Cecilia do not say, in the sense of reveal, is not merely a lack of speech; they often appear as silent victims because they are denied the legitimacy *of* name and the authority *to* name. Denied legitimate speech, the female heroine must resort to hysteria which speaks "of an impossible and also a forbidden speech . . . It speaks as *symptoms* of an 'it can't speak to or about itself'" (*TSNO,* 136; ellipses in text).

Burney discloses the symptoms of forbidden speech at those "unspeakable" points of crisis in her novels. Cecilia's madness, Camilla's sickness, even Evelina's anguish over the purloined letter cry out for us to reconsider woman's hysteria as belonging to the crucial issue of namelessness as a phenomenon of language. Like Burney's Miss Nobody, a person who is not a person, these narratives suggest that namelessness is the silent condition of individual women, who when represented by the name Woman, must speak only with the borrowed voice of Man. When the identity of a woman is not derived from concrete experience, from her genuine existential condition, then the conceptual name stands in front of and obscures as it represents. And when the woman, like the Wanderer is "unknown, unnamed," something even more radical happens; name, the very process of naming itself becomes a phenomenality, no longer obscured under the concepts assigned by the patriarchal.

If, as Julia Epstein suggests, namelessness is the condition of Burney's women, then as no-name, a woman is nothing in the sense that she has not been fittingly spoken by those who have named her.[4] But namelessness is also a space for what is absent, opening up the possibility for a woman to come into the unconcealment of person. While those in authority speak *for* Woman, namelessness lets a woman speak herself. As unknown and unnamed, Incognita (identity disguised or concealed; incognition, not knowable) can call into being, name what did not exist before, not even as an object of intellection or imagination, and that "wandering" name, fluid and plural, is her own. *The Wanderer* focuses on the simultaneous revealing and concealing inherent in the process of naming. Far from constituting a woman as a named, passive object, namelessness discloses her as a human agent.

If Burney merely duplicates in this work the inhibiting structures governing women's communication within society, then her rhetorical movement seems to yield to the inexpressible and find refuge in silence.[5] But to describe Burney's strategy in this novel as a rebellion against propriety effectually places Burney in the ideological camp of the fabricators of prohibition.[6] What constitutes female liberty is graphically contrasted in the characters of Juliet and Elinor and helps to explain why Juliet is so often seen as the passive sufferer and Elinor as the active revolutionary. However, it is not the revolutionary Elinor who is the heroine of the story and title, but the extremely proper Juliet, whose actions cannot successfully be described as rebellious. Both women struggle with prohibition, but their responses to it are radically different.[7]

How do these women liberate themselves from the cultural prohibition against speaking their own discourse without engaging in the patriarchal discourse that fabricates prohibition? Julia Kristeva says that "as long as any libertarian movement, feminism included, does not analyze its own relationship to power and does not renounce belief in its own identity it remains capable of being coopted . . . by power."[8] Kristeva warns that only when the antinomic understanding of action (as opposite of passivity) is dismantled, by no longer being tied to gender, will prohibition itself be de-centered.

In order to see *The Wanderer* as other than "female difficulties," the antinomic thinking which privileges aggressive action and denigrates nonaction as passivity must be dismantled. In other words, the interpretive position from which one reads the novel and the political stance from which one responds to cultural prohibition are interrelated. This interrelationship is the realm of language as an event of human vision. Since envisioning involves speech, it is also an event of conceptualizing and hence naming. As Marxist critics well understand, the struggle over language by any new order means claiming cherished terms (i.e., passive, active) and narratives (i.e., gender myths) for itself. In this case, a narrative of woman's namelessness brings us full circle into the conflict between the prevailing understanding of language as designator-thing versus language as a narrative revealing.

We are immediately plunged into the enigma of the Wanderer in the opening chapter when a mysterious, disguised female pleads with the pilot of a boat to give her safe passage from the terror in France to refuge in England. The narrator says that "her name, her connexions, her actual situation, and her object in making the voyage, resisted enquiry, eluded insinuation, and baffled conjecture."[9] The young, bandaged stranger seems foreign; furthermore, she is traveling alone. Rather than inviting sympathy for her obvious distress, the weary traveler arouses mistrust and censure from most of the English passengers on the boat. This female "Ænigma" appears to the other English passengers as "the blackest, dirtiest, raggedest wretch," a "glaring imposter," "wandering Creole" (1:85). She further provokes their antipathy, indeed cruelty, when she is unable to account for herself and gently but firmly refuses to name herself. Mrs. Maple, a mean-spirited, imperious dowager, commands the "Incognita" to "let me only know who you are, and I shall myself be the best judge what should be done for you. What is it, then, once for all, that you call yourself? No prevarications! Tell me your name, or go about your business" (1:116).

Right from the start Burney presents us with a mystery involving the name of a woman. Like Burney's women who are nameless in the representational sense, the heroine of *The Wanderer* has no place except as an abstraction, a "generalized other."[10] Without a surname signifying her own culture, Juliet Granville, as she is later called, cannot be socially acceptable. Since the social world depicted in the novel decides who is nameable, just as surname designates who belongs to a family, Juliet's namelessness makes her alienation culturally absolute.

Why does Juliet refuse to name herself when to do so would allay suspicion and arouse sympathy—especially if her plight were told? We can approach the paradox that denying name is also the possibility of naming by borrowing an analogy from Lacan's clinical experience. In the famous case of the bleeding woman, the analyst, without explanation, prohibits the analysand from discourse on her bleeding, and wonderfully, the bleeding stops. The analyst's prohibition says that the subject of the bleeding woman's speech is the woman herself and not this mere symptom of her "illness." In other words, the bleeding "declares" that the woman cannot speak except by addressing this symptom as its subject. Thus, the woman is always deprived of speech. The analyst directs herself not toward the woman's neurotic suffering, her bleeding, but toward her existential suffering, a lack of discourse. By means of her injunction against speaking a "neurotic" discourse, the analyst offers the woman a more authentic access to speech.[11] In the same way and unlike the earlier works, *The Wanderer* addresses not just the symptoms of the suffering "Incognita," her hysteria—but woman herself. The narrative, by telling the story of the one who lacks discourse, gives her access to speech in the forum once denied her—the public world.

Incognita's name is revealed after three volumes, and the story of her background even later, when Juliet seeks refuge from two interrelated "reigns" of terror: a forced marriage and the French Revolution. Her husband is a sadistic French official who marries her merely to obtain her portion of the Granville family inheritance. The document proving Juliet's legitimacy and right to the Granville fortune, like Evelina's purloined letter, is stolen by the French official. This document is Juliet's only proof that she is indeed the eldest Granville daughter, that she has the legitimacy that incarnates patrilineal power, that she has a right to say her name. Her name has meaning to others only insofar as its worth is calculable. Juliet's document proves she is worth five thousand pounds. Hence her name represents a material denomination for those who demand the world be put in order and reckoned according to exchange value. When she appears in disguise and conceals her name, she invites others to designate her "nameless," and "worthless." She is doubly concealed, first by herself as "Incognita" and second by those who negatively designate her as nothing. They fail to see the person before them, their vision blinded by a social mechanism which causes their primary relationship to the world to be that of reification.[12] Those who ruthlessly name her nameless conceal her with all the passion of their will-to-power more than she conceals herself in the disguise of "Incognita."

Juliet escapes to England only to live under the constant fear that she will be discovered, named, and disclosed to the evil officer of Robespierre. She dares not even apply for aid to her beloved, aristocratic foster family in France out of fear for their safety, nor, because of her perilous situation, can she apply to her friends or the Granville family in England. Although Juliet is of English parentage on both sides, the marriage of her genteel mother to her

aristocratic father has never been publicly acknowledged or recognized. In England itself Juliet may be free from the amoral evils of
the French Revolution, but in decorum-bound English society she
is beset by cruel, selfish women and rapacious, cavalier men dili-
gently intent upon uncovering what they think is hidden under her
virtuous appearance and behavior. Juliet's silence about her history,
her family, her upbringing, makes her into a no-thing, inaccessible
to a hegemony of name because "unrepresentable."

Juliet's namelessness invites those who seek to penetrate her deceptive appearance to affirm what they already believe—that she is
the embodiment of "double dealing, false appearances, and lurking
disguise" (1:415). The episodic plot follows Juliet's female difficulties
and the countless machinations of those eager, perhaps even driven,
to penetrate her appearance and discover the hidden reality beneath,
to find out who she is: "Unprotected, unsustained, unknown. Her
situation was mysterious, and seemed open, at times, to the most
alarming suspicions; though the unequivocal regularity and propriety
of her conduct, snatched her from any positive calumny" (2:296).
A late eighteenth-century culture, firmly allied to Cartesian doubt
and the empiricist dualism of appearance and reality, even more
firmly believes that all appearances are subject to question, assault,
and penetration—no matter how much Juliet's appearance or actions
speak of her integrity. She exclaims, "Must slander lie in wait, to
misconstrue the most simple actions, by surmising the most culpable
designs?" (3:216). As Nancy K. Miller says, the not so hidden agenda
for discovering "woman" by many eighteenth-century thinkers is
"to discover Man" who projects her like a veil.[13]

An appearance-reality model demands hunting for the truth behind deceptive appearances. Mr. Riley sums up the unslaked appetite of those eager to "see through" Juliet when he says, "I have
long had a craving desire to know who this girl is" (4:221). For
others, her mystery is a source of fascination and allurement: "Who,
who, thought [Harleigh] again, cans't thou be? And why . . . thus
friendless—thus desolate—thus mysterious?" (1:224). Or again from
the elderly playboy Sir Jasper: "Tell me, then, who you are, resistless
paragon! and you shall wander no more in this nameless state, an
exquisite, but nearly visionary being!" (4:159). Some constantly ask
Juliet who she is, as though in knowing her name they could single-
handedly classify her and cause her human essence to come into

being. Since Juliet has no documents, no form of accurate, verifiable speech bearing the consensus of a truth statement, she seems inherently false.

Juliet sadly but resignedly chides herself: "Must she quarrel with her benefactors, because they gave not implicit credit to the word of a lonely Wanderer" (1:151). The word "wander" stresses both the absence of a fixed course or goal and the inability to express oneself clearly and coherently. "Wander" also implies deviation from proper behavior or going astray. Like the appearance of the earlier Burney heroines at points of intense crisis, Juliet appears to others without the boundaries of a fixed course, in other words without the guidance of male intellect and patriarchal directive that would lend her word credibility. Like Evelina, Juliet has only the truth of herself written in an appearing that seems incoherent, aimless, and thereby improper.

The demand to know Juliet's name is actually a desire on the part of society to hear the communal narrative that her name would represent. To tell her "story," that is, to make coherent and intelligible the mystery of her entry as a "newcomer" into their world, Juliet does not, as they believe, need a material or economic denomination to designate her. As shown earlier, naming is not the arbitrary imposition by a subject designating an object; rather naming is a revelatory event: "*who* somebody is . . . we can know only by knowing the story of which [she] is [her]self the hero . . . everything else we know of [her] . . . tells us only *what* [she] is or was."[14]

The basic error of those in the novel who are incapable—to use the famous words of Keats—"of being in uncertainties, Mysteries, doubts, without any irritable reaching after fact & reason"[15]—those characters are committed to the veridical in that they overlook the inevitability with which Juliet discloses herself as a distinct and unique person. This is true even when they are wholly bent upon negating her story, of reaching an altogether essentialist classification of her. Name even as nameless has a narrative, revelatory character:

> The disclosure of the "who" through speech, and the setting of a new beginning through action, always fall into an already existing web where their immediate consequences can be felt. Together they start a new process which eventually emerges as the unique life story of the newcomer, affecting uniquely the life

stories of all those with whom he comes into contact. It is because
of this already existing web . . . in which action alone is real, that
it "produces" stories with or without intention. (Arendt, *HC,* 184)

Juliet introduces the unpredictable and unknowable into an already
existing narrative—a narrative whose outcome the others wish to
keep in their control.

Juliet, without the twofold protection of family and property (the
family-owned private share in the world), without the rights of mem-
bership in a social class (a societal substitute for family), consequently, without even a story she can tell or a past to account for
her, must throw herself upon the often meager benevolence of others.
She describes her woeful circumstances as follows:

> My situation is now deplorable indeed!—I have no letter, no di-
> rection from the person whom I had hoped to meet; and whose
> abode, whose address, I know not how to discover! I must not
> apply to any of my original friends: unknown, and in circum-
> stances the most strange, if not suspicious, can I hope to make
> myself any new ones? . . . yet dare not say who, nor what I am,—
> and hardly even know it myself. (1:135)

She bears no letter, no sign, or pointer to direct her. To others she
bears no sign with which they can arbitrarily categorize her or assign
her her value. Juliet's only instructions are to "seek, then, unnamed
and unknown, during this dread interval of separation, to reside
with some worthy and happy family, whose social felicity may bring,
at least, reflected happiness to your own breast" (1:277, 278). It is
no wonder Juliet feels herself "though in my native country, like a
helpless foreigner; unknown, unprotected, and depending solely
upon the benevolence of those by whom, accidentally, I am seen,
for kindness,—or even for support!—" (2:46).

Without a surname that identifies and legitimizes Juliet within
the familial context of culture, and without even a given name to
individuate her, Juliet cannot be placed in the context of class, family,
social rule ("though in my native country, like a helpless foreigner").
All the various relationships that bind one to culture, that give human
beings definition by forming the limits within which they can act
and take their shape—these are unavailable to her in her own native
country. Without these limits, Juliet appears to others without

bounds and devoid of authority, thereby inviting curiosity, interrogation, and attack. Without a narrative to explain her namelessness, Juliet's difference alienates her from the common world and separates her perspective from the normative way of apprehending the world.

The female as depicted in this novel cannot be separated from the theory that constitutes "woman" as a concept: "The term 'concept' is . . . essentially a dummy expression or variable, whose meaning is assignable only in the context of a theory, and cannot be independently ascertained."[16] The female is identified by metaphysical positings, by "traits," "attributes," "roles," or even biology. To be so named is to be rendered mute in a world voiced only by this model. For the human to be represented by the representative name of "woman" is to speak only with the borrowed voice of the male; in effect, it is to be silenced.

Unlike the world of the earlier novels, this society is not merely decorum-bound; it is rife with individuals who try to exert a will-to-power over others by silencing them. They invoke the rationale of the social contract in which individual opinion is autonomous and all other opinion a threat to that autonomy.

Juliet's experiences do not relate to a Hobbesian understanding of significant human action, and from that perspective it is difficult to see her behavior as anything but the stereotype for passivity. Though the others in the novel see Juliet's inassertiveness as inviting attack, *they* are determined, even in their determination to make her either an actor or a victim, by their responses to her. In such a case, her inaction, provoking and drawing their (re)action, cannot be properly labeled "passive." She conquers by attraction rather than aggression, recognizing that her very presence, more than any purposive self-assertion on her part, becomes the new standard by which all others are tested.

Juliet reveals her agency within the intersubjective actions that reveal her character. If speech only asserts or states, then the speech of Incognita, an alien other, reveals nothing. Juliet's namelessness frustrates those egos who cannot name and dispose of her as a thing. Accordingly, several old, embittered women delight in publicly humiliating Juliet and in using her namelessness as an excuse for venting their wrath and imposing their whims.

A society that is not only rigid in its morals but paranoid in its fear of change fortifies itself by an entrenched response to uncertainty, whether in the form of the "evils" of the French Revolution

and its "heretical" principles or in the threat to order that is sym-
bolized by the "double dealing, false appearances and lurking disguise" of a woman "without a family she dare claim, without a
story she dare tell, without a name she dare avow" (1:414, 415).
Especially the females express repressed bitterness, jealousy, and
outrage toward Juliet because they link accomplishments and name
to exchange value. Elinor chides Harleigh that in loving Juliet he
is infatuated with "mystery" and "the marvellous and obscure"
(1:412). Certainly Juliet's mysterious and silent appearing disrupts
many preconceived opinions. Those who are uneasy about what the
mysterious woman might change in the social world, who reason in
the form of reckoning with consequences, wish to exclude contingency from human affairs.

The power of Juliet's silence and inaction provokes violence from
other women. Mrs. Maple begrudgingly agrees to take Juliet into
her home under the urging of the independent and spirited Elinor
but stubbornly maintains—in spite of Juliet's graces—that this
"foundling girl" is an "illegitimate stroller, who does not so much
as know her own name" (1:183). Namelessness implies chaos, and
the horrors of illegitimacy, duplicity, and design. She hides Juliet
away in a garret as an example of her benevolence and is most
chagrined when time and again she must allow Juliet converse in
high society. When Juliet's home stage performance captivates the
attention and friendship of the aristocratic Lord Melbury and Lady
Aurora, Mrs. Ireton relents in her plan to cast Juliet upon the streets.
Mrs. Howel imperiously focuses upon Juliet's namelessness as a
form of crime. These female viragos feel personally affronted that
Juliet appears in all instances so obviously cultivated, and that "her
language, her air, and her manner, pervading every disadvantage
of apparel, poverty, and subjection, had announced her, from the
first, to have received the education . . . of a gentlewoman." They
use the issue of namelessness and its attendant threat of the unexpected as a license for revenge in order to secure for themselves
absolute sovereignty. Juliet's "looks so speaking; grace so silent"
provoke their fury even when she doesn't "utter a word." These
social arbiters invoke the cultural norms in order to allow their
passions full sway. Juliet says that they are women filled with their
own sensibility and have no sensibility left for others.

Other female characters pretend to aid Juliet merely in order to call attention to themselves, to impress others, and to gain social advantage. Juliet observes that the genteel women are cruel because they have never known distress (3:53), that their pity in hiring her is self-gratifying, and that their so-called benevolence produces no remuneration for the services she renders (3:55). Even Elinor's kindness toward Juliet, based partially on curiosity and pique, is the result of her being "so completely governed by impulse; and . . . her passions as her guides to glory" (1:432). Finally, each one of these women in her self-indulgent isolation practices a form of rule that defies community while pretending to invoke its authority. This practice is commonly called tyranny.

The tyranny of these women provokes a reign of terror against Juliet. Mrs. Ireton, after hiring Juliet as a "companion," uses namelessness as a pretext to tyrannize over this "mere nothing" with criticism, taunts, and irony. Montesquieu realized, however, that the most outstanding characteristic of tyranny is not power, but isolation.[17] The tyrant isolates himself from his subjects, and the subjects isolate themselves from one another through mutual fear. The tyrant rules as one against all, and this "all" includes everyone who, in the presence of the tyrant, is, or seems to be, powerless. Tyranny sows the seeds of impotence, for fear prevents others from overtly aiding Juliet. In answering the dowager's demands, Juliet provokes this retort about her namelessness: "'Called?' repeated Mrs. Ireton; 'what do you mean by called?—who calls you?—What are you called for?—Why do you wait to be called?—And where are you called from?'" (3:237).

Vengeance abounds in this novel as a reaction that shrinks the possibility for action. The will to command in these household tyrants, far from being a characteristic of the strong, is a vice of the weak. Their revenge continues, rather than extirpates, the transgression of namelessness; it reduces the others' ability to act and binds them to its process. Mrs. Howel, after discovering that Lady Aurora's guest is a "nobody," demands an explanation from Juliet and, not receiving one, banishes her, to prevent further access to the Granvilles. Still refusing to acknowledge Juliet's pedigree without absolute proof, she publicly accuses her of thievery, and in effect, orchestrates her own estrangement from the Granvilles.

Incognita's demonstrable innocence provides no escape from such
tyranny; rather, as our discussion of *Evelina* revealed, the cultural
norm of female innocence-passivity, far from being a refuge, is part
of the dialectical play that invites willful tyranny. In contrast to
Evelina however, Juliet knows that the appearance of innocence-
passivity not only invites "ill will" but that most of the men she
encounters are eager to accost her and test her modesty. It is Juliet's
understanding of the dialectic within passivity that prevents her from
falling into the role of unwitting victim. She comments, "How much
the charm, though not the worth, of innocence depends upon manners" (4:334). In other words, the charm of innocence is a social
construction and not a state of being. She understands that sincerity
of motive cannot make her innocent, that the interpretive force of
her purity of heart depends upon the community. When young Lord
Melbury assumes that she is a courtesan in spite of her friendship
with his sister, her impeccable behavior, and his own firsthand ob-
servances of her, Juliet asks him with great dignity, why, with a
sister as pure as his, he cannot think "other females may be exempt,
at least from depravity" (1:320).

For Juliet, namelessness is a concrete condition enabling her to
understand that innocence, assumable as "the essence of the female,"
is assailed for the same reason that namelessness provokes attack.
Both are fantasies of something hidden that invite penetration. That
is, Juliet's actual namelessness is the paradigmatic, but unrecog-
nized, condition of the earlier heroines as females. Evelina, Cecilia,
and Camilla, enmeshed in the "system of masculine representations"
by their differentiation as "woman," appear "nameless." Furthermore, because they lack the authority to name, we see them as
passive, voiceless, or hysteric—other "names" for woman. Juliet's
experiences as "unnamed, unknown," provide her with ample existential evidence that her social condition entails all that is dark,
riddlesome, and deceptive. The nameless does not stand as an equal
entity opposed to the named or nameable but as the dark, negative,
undesirable version of this antinomy. For all of Juliet's difficulties,
and they are legion, none is greater than "the unremitting necessity
of seeming always impenetrable" (5:367).

Juliet arouses social tyranny in women and sexual tyranny in
men. They see a nameless female as inviting and deserving their
advances. Trapped within a system of masculine representations that

circumscribe her actions and dictate her propriety, Juliet wonders whether "it is only under the domestic roof,—that roof to me denied—that woman can know safety, respect and honour?" (4:253). As long as she lacks the protection of (sur)name, the patriarchal guardianship over woman or the metaphoric "domestic roof" that is to her "denied," Juliet knows that her actions will be misinterpreted. Overhearing Sir Lyell's lascivious intentions toward her, Juliet feels horror "from her inability to shew her resentment" (3:159).

Some of the men know that the rules guaranteed to protect a woman by limiting her parameters promote a kind of unrestrained freedom. Thus when Juliet is ostracized at a concert by the women because she inhabits the in-between position of a music teacher (somewhere between gentry and shopgirl), the fact that "she should appear, and remain, thus strangely alone in public, marked her" in Sir Lyell's eyes "as easy prey" (2:128). Juliet appears "without respect" in his eyes, but understands clearly nonetheless, that what some men wish to adore they also wish to demolish (2:122).

Hence Juliet, precisely because she is nameless, often finds herself appearing as what others expect to see rather than what they *do* see. Miss Arbe mistakenly thinks that Incognita's name is "Miss Ellis" (L.S.), an appellation that sticks to Juliet during the course of the novel even though it is not her real name. This mistake exemplifies how others arbitrarily misname Juliet rather than consent to her appearing as she is. Her namelessness veils her in the sense that the culture she inhabits is unwilling to see her. What people do see when they see her depends on invisible veils of expectation that cover her with their personal prejudices.

Since Juliet's silence is self-imposed, she concludes that deliberately concealing her name and history draws from others an assumption that she is false: "Involved as I am in darkness and obscurity, she cried, ought I to expect milder judgment? No! I have no right to complain. Appearances are against me; and to appearances are we not all either victims or dupes?" (2:197). Only a few, like Harleigh, are willing to believe what Juliet's appearance speaks "from the ease with which she wore her ornaments, the grace with which she set them off, the elegance of her deportment, and an air of dignified modesty, that spoke her not only accustomed to such attire, but also to the good breeding and refined manners, which announce the habits of life to have been formed in the superiour classes of society" (1:199). Harleigh enlightens Lord Melbury about Juliet's character by asking him to consider how "a female, who is young, beautiful and accomplished, can suffer from pecuniary distress, if her character be not unimpeachable?" (1:337).

In contrast to Evelina and Camilla, Juliet realizes that her namelessness and silence mark her for others as a person "without bounds." Whoever learns unthinkingly to perceive a nameless, unprotected female as a "swindler" or a whore will find it almost impossible to see her as virtuous. Thus without a past Juliet's negative "inheritance" marks her lack of the testament to select and name, to hand down and preserve, to confer worth from the abyss of history. To others this lack threatens continuity, leaving only the potential for chaos. Nonetheless, those who are confronted with Juliet's "darkness and obscurity" act and illuminate themselves in response to the void of her namelessness.

Unlike her predecessors in the earlier novels, Juliet recognizes the pitfalls for one who has no part in the making of meaning that narrates a culture's history. She understands that "all public appeals are injurious to female fame," that a female is "utterly dependant [sic] upon situation—connexions—circumstance," that her conduct is "criticised, not scrutinized; her character is censured, not examined; her labours are unhonoured, and her qualifications are but lures to ill will!" (2:197). She is consistently thwarted in her attempts at gainful employment.

Juliet's demeanor, however, does persuade the quietly sympathetic Harleigh that she is genteel and cultivated in spite of her peculiar situation, deficient means, and lack of recommendation. He says, "I think her . . . an elegant and well bred young woman, under some extraordinary and inexplicable difficulties: for there is a modesty in her air, which art, though it might attain, could not support; and a dignity in her conduct in refusing all succour . . . that make it impossible for me to have any doubt upon the fairness of her character" (1:159). Harleigh becomes Juliet's quiet champion. He fends off suspicion against her by appealing to a revelatory rather than verifiable truth when he says, "I can defend no single particular, even to myself; but yet the whole, the all-together, carries with it an indescribable, but irresistible vindication" (1:48). In fact, it is Harleigh who eloquently speaks for the other side of representation when he says that it is by her suffering (in Irigaray's terms by an "it can't speak to or for itself") that Juliet *does* reveal herself even though this form of proof may be "thought insufficient by the world" (1:186). He makes this plea for her: "She is unknown to us; except by her distresses; and these . . . call loudly for our sympathy and assistance, and through the propriety of her conduct, lay claim to our respect" (1:186). Like Lacan's bleeding woman, Juliet is known only by the symptoms of her suffering.

In spite of Harleigh's obvious kindness and impeccable behavior, Juliet adamantly refuses all aid, understanding that her unprotected status provides for the grossest misinterpretation of her behavior—and for the subtlest encouragement to misinterpretation. Harleigh falls in love with Juliet and asks her to marry him, not knowing who she is or that she is already married. Juliet laments that in this dilemma she is doomed "to seek—so hardly—the support that flies me,—yet to fly the consolation that offers" (2:251). Distress forces her to use his resources, though it will encourage the perseverance of a rejected man. She laments that woman is "pronounced upon only from outward semblance:—and indeed, what other criterion has the world? Can it read the heart?" (2:367).

When asking, "Can it read the heart?" Juliet recalls for us the question of sensibility that confronted Camilla and baffled Edgar. Those who reify "Incognita" exclude from their judgment their own heartfelt assumptions. That is, the basis for relations between people becomes "thing-like," acquires an illusory objectivity, and conceals all traces of relatedness. As the discussion of *Camilla* showed, this form of sensibility is unspeakable under patriarchal restraint and the representational norm for language. And as Kristeva and Irigaray claim, since woman instinctively feels that it is through her sensibility that she first becomes acquainted with a wholeness of presence radically different from conceptualized identities, she lets hysteric discourse speak for her. Juliet cannot presume upon the certitude available to others. Harleigh, at least, openly attends to Juliet in a mode of respect—an openness that can best be described as alien to ruling, measuring, and subsuming another. Harleigh's knowledge of Juliet—his understanding of her integrity without knowing her name and story, his belief that he knows her by her distresses—gives credence to a deeply felt but not articulated experience. Based upon respect, regard admires more than a person's traits, talents, faculties; it attends openly to the person in a manner

that is mutually revelatory and communally shaped. Whether she
has a name or not, Juliet cannot prevent disclosure of herself to one
who is attuned to her. Juliet recognizes that Harleigh is open to her:
"He knows me to be indigent . . . yet does not conclude me open to
corruption! He sees me friendless and unprotected,—yet offers me
no indignity!" (1:315). The lack of openness in others determines the
degree of narrowness and obscurity implied by Juliet's namelessness.

Juliet's lament that no one except Harleigh gives credit to the
word of a lonely wanderer indicates that, for a woman, an ever
present source of pain is the inability to speak, to give coherence
to the otherwise random exigencies that sweep over her. This unarticulated experience causes a woman pain—a pain that can sometimes only be expressed in hysteric discourse (as with the bleeding
woman) but also one that *can* speak out of the place where these
bonds most deeply touch her. Heidegger's commentary on pain in
The End of Philosophy explains that suffering is only a passive im-
mobility if understood as receiving an action without initiating one
in return. Suffering can't transform thinking if "it is only experienced as suffering, as passive, and thus as the opposite state of
action" (102, 110). In other words, woman's suffering, understood in
the usual reductive way as inherently passive, will always be a mere
symptom or sensation that obscures and narrows the disclosive power
of suffering. Juliet's pain makes her keenly aware of what she neither
possesses nor controls, herself and contingency. She may be the
rightful heir to the Granville estate, but she has no proof that would
validate her. Those who persecute her suffer as well: they suffer a
lack of need in confidently thinking that they do know the truth of
her being.

II

We have come to a point of great promise and great danger. What
follows will seem, in terms of traditional categories, to be a return,
with little or no difference, to the stereotyped passivity of the feminine. One who is open to the flux of being; who figures an open-
ended becoming, which positively is the infinite variety of the diaries'
"Nobody" and negatively the capricious Camilla; who lives for her
husband like Evelina; whose final scene, like Cecilia's, is Virtue—
such a woman sounds like the old clichés of Western patriarchal

discourse. Furthermore, to repeat the Hegelian argument that the slave is freer than the master can be read as a consent to one's shackles that promotes the status quo. But, and this is an important but, if we are to make the needed advance in thinking on this point, that is, to disrupt the patriarchal-antipatriarchal antinomy, it is important to broaden our approach to the general problem of pain and action in relation to Juliet's suffering. To do so, we must reconsider the phenomenon of sensibility.

To see Burney as offering *either* sentiment *or* aggressive confrontation hypostatizes both sentiment and action. To say for example, that women console but rarely spur to action, posits the suffering subject as the receiver of sensations existing passively in a state of feeling, posits the active agent as lacking any attunement to the full context of action.[18] The language open to the one is hysteric discourse; that available to the other is the discourse of representation. A sensibility unavailable to consciousness—not for that reason (as Descartes insisted) necessarily inferior or 'confused'—"thinks" in the sense that it holds open a heightened awareness of being alive (sentiment in the old sense) and a heightened sense of the web of background relations in which one acts. This is indeed the traditional crucible of pain not proved false by its contradicting consistent cultural practice. Juliet's unremitting pain can be understood as merely the use of sensation to "outbid reality and bribe sensibilities" or as the truest of messages, a *history* of tears.[19] The latter history rereads Juliet's suffering as forcing her to accept the world as it is and not as she wishes it to be. Her namelessness opens her to risk that she confronts, paradoxically, by yielding to a destiny she cannot escape: "She was, a stranger to security, subject to dismission, at the mercy of accident, and at the will of caprice" (3:178).

A woman's felt response to the specific afflictions characteristic of her position historically situates her creative and critical action. To insert herself into an already narrated world and begin a story of her own bespeaks an act of commitment to world and history—its political narrative. Juliet changes the narrative of her world simply by being the story *she is*. Her story is open, without an ending, without *arche* and *telos*, and unlike the narrative she enters. "Incognita," or namelessness, signals an opening to possibility, to nam*ing* in contrast to the stasis of being named. When Juliet is assailed and deliberately humiliated, the narrator says it serves to disclose her courage: "For courage, where there is any nobleness of mind, always rises highest, when oppressive pride seeks to crush it by studied humiliation" (1:292).

Juliet's affliction is the wellspring of her action and a source of wonder, an unforeseeable event to those who oppress her. A case in point is her response to malicious attacks. Mrs. Ireton uses a private fete as an opportunity to mortify Juliet before an audience. Even though Juliet cries out against the exactions of "prudence upon feeling," she reflects that "in her present dependent condition . . . she ought to yield" (3:314). Further commands from Mrs. Ireton are so imperious that Juliet would depart the household were she not prevented by the guests. Harangued again, Juliet endures further humiliation in total silence, "convinced that where all authority is on the side of the aggressor, resistance only provokes added triumph" (3:323). Even those sympathetic toward Juliet are reluctant to defend her under the tyranny of Mrs. Ireton. She maliciously assails Juliet to the point of making her seem a "toad eater"—until Ireton's arrogance "awakens spirit" and Juliet moves firmly and silently toward the door. When Mrs. Ireton demands, "Permit me to enquire *who* told you to go?" Juliet's quiet, spontaneous response neither retaliates nor defends. And yet, Mrs. Ireton is defeated by the force of her own attack when Juliet replies, "A person, Madam, who has not the honour to be known to you,—myself!" (3:350).

Conflict and indeterminancy enable Juliet to discover herself, to test her understanding not by a set of rules that everyone can follow, but by what answers for her. The fitness of her act accommodates her promise not to name herself, accommodates both her personal sense of dignity and the social order. In this respect her action is spontaneous as well as distinctive. It is truly political and historical in its response—political in that it places her in some relation to the other that binds them together, historical in that she takes up her past (i.e., namelessness) as the sole site of possibility ("a person . . . who has not the honour to be known to you") for the future. She narrates when she begins to become who she might be. She acts toward a possibility that fulfills the past in the future. In this case her past is possibility itself and narrativity the essence of her action. The contrast between Ireton and Juliet at this point reveals the *meaning* of action as disclosure, revelation.

Juliet's response demonstrates that speech *is* action; it confounds everyone by provoking general surprise and "universal demand of who the young person might be, and what she could mean" (3:351). In relinquishing any attempt to defend herself Juliet opens herself to other perspectives and lets her own be assimilated to them. This renunciation enables her to forego a demand for retribution. And foregoing aggression redeems her *act* as more than simply excusing a person or assenting to deeds that destroy one's personal integrity. This freeing action is not without danger, for "at the will of caprice," Juliet finds freedom to be "a source of perpetual difficulty and instability" (3:178, 181). However, in this act, Juliet also discovers she "had the world to begin again" (3:181).

Having the world to begin again enables Juliet to authenticate her identity as an ongoing possibility. She does not merely re-act but acts anew and unexpectedly, unconditioned by Mrs. Ireton's malice. Her act does not, like Mrs. Ireton's, attempt to abolish difference, creating a social order in which otherness, Juliet's name-lessness, is nonexistent. Such an action masks another kind of power play, alienating one from desire in an attempt to present oneself as a cultural paragon. Revenge or reaction against a previous action continues an action but does not reverse it. For this reason Juliet's response temporarily alters the narrative and spontaneously casts her in a new situation. Unexpectedly altering the world is not a purposive or aim-directed action, but neither is it inaction.

However passive Juliet may seem at times, her deeds must be set within the larger context of her nameless position. She is in England by her deliberate choice and direct action; she has chosen to resist the claims upon her made by her false husband in France; she has chosen her own way of eluding his snares as well as those of others; she has chosen not to reveal her name at any cost. Her choices are tested in actions; her deeds correspond to her words. What Juliet does not do is intellectualize—she does not ponder the rightness or wrongness of her act either before or after it. She does not deploy her mind as a perversion of it as the others do, in service to her ego.

Juliet's dependency forces her to discover another vocabulary to say herself; namelessness acts to re-word the world. In fact, re-word-ing the world in word and deed *is* action in its most deeply traditional

sense.[20] The lexicon of Juliet's world, though hampered by patriarchal restraint, is her means for understanding herself. She is not self-
made; she is not a Lear railing against the universe. She fully accepts
the split between her speaking act and what others hear. Reading her
world, she discovers what she shall be called. "Calling" implies a
state of attentiveness, of openness toward the way in which beings are
heard. Accordingly, it is by means of an injunction against naming
herself that she finds access to speech. Thus, Juliet shows us that silence itself is a special mode of speaking and being heard.

For the very reason that we, as beings immersed in our Western,
patriarchal culture, still see action as making a product, whether
fashioning a self or performing deeds, Juliet's character will be
judged as more acted upon than acting. But if Juliet's action can
be seen as yielding to human destiny and renouncing traditional
notions of authority and subjectivity, then she exemplifies all the
potential that Burney imagines in her play with "Nobody"—a subject
of infinite displacement. In other words, namelessness, together with
a personal obligation to conceal it for the sake of other perspectives,
forces Juliet to reflect upon events, upon herself, upon the consequences of her actions. Her quest to name herself is not for the sake
of indulging desires, but for the sake of finding the boundaries that
liberate her from the socially predetermined self. As she says to
Harleigh, "I cannot consider myself to be my own" (5:166).

Though Juliet's silent response to events is traditional, in the
sense of properly "feminine," and though she seems exasperatingly
perfect—Harleigh asks, "Why not exile now, and repudiate for ever,
that terrible rigour of reserve that has so long been at war with your
humanity?"—a pejorative reading of her behavior is also traditional.
Nevertheless, Juliet's behavior can be seen as traditional in another
sense: she has fully assimilated the tradition that, to the degree it
fits her, is fitting for her.

Though others would deny Juliet a past, she herself knows she
has one. She is linked to the past because her present ability to act
at all partakes of actions that stretch backward and forward, actions
that make her historical. We know of her life in France and of her
ongoing need to conceal herself. Harleigh describes our link to past
and future when he says that there are "ties from which we are
never emancipated; ties which cling to our nature, and which, though
voluntary, are imperious, and cannot be broken or relinquished

without self-reproach; ties formed by the equitable laws of fellow-feeling; which bind us to our family, which unite us with our friends; and which, by our own expectations, teach us what is due to our connexions" (2:354). Most of the ties that bind people together are already given when the individual appears in the world; others are initiated by promises mutually contracted.[21] Without both ties to the past and an ability to initiate promises, Juliet would literally *be* the nothing that her namelessness makes her seem.

Elinor upbraids Juliet for what she considers to be a slavish allegiance to traditional female roles, forgetting that without those ties Juliet would be a nothing, no one. If Juliet were not true to promises made, she would betray her own integrity. It is easy for Elinor to advocate iconoclasm when her position—she is independently wealthy—frees her from the very necessity that weighs upon Juliet.

From a sense of responsibility toward Elinor, Juliet acts as go-between to Harleigh in spite of her instinctive decorum and reserve. Juliet's own feelings for Harleigh make her situation even more painful: "Ellis could not utter a word: every phrase she could suggest seemed to teem with danger; yet she felt that her silence could not but indicate the truth which it sought to hide" (1:383). Even the traditional Harleigh argues with Juliet to forget her promise, abandon her scrupulous reserve, and confide in him. Juliet answers by pointing out that if she were to tell him her story and break the silence she promised to keep, she would not only lose her self-respect, but his respect as well.

Juliet has bound herself in promising her foster family in France to conceal her name and remain silent. In acting on behalf of others she is acting on behalf of who she is. Harleigh finally learns about her marriage and past and begs her not to return to France with her so-called husband. Juliet replies:

Dread and atrocious as is my connection, my faith to it must be unbroken . . . till the iniquity of my chains may be proved, and my restoration to my violated freedom may be legalized. . . . Little as I feel to belong to the person in question, I cannot consider myself to be my own! 'Tis a tie which, whether or not it binds me to him, excludes me, while thus circumstanced [*sic*], from all others! (5:166)

Her tie is not merely an externally imposed, legal bond (her forced marriage); rather, it is a past event that she cannot deny, excluding her in the present from a similar tie. That is, Juliet cannot consider herself to be her own because of a tie that precludes her acting against it. Although she loves Harleigh, she will not consider the claims of her ego for happiness or for any consideration of her inheritance. She is not in flight from responsiblility; she does not, like Elinor, act ahistorically out of the preeminence of passion. Juliet will submit to the outrageous demand of the French official and sacrifice herself, not for reasons of law, for it is obvious to the English that her marriage is illegal, but for the sake of her own integrity. By the same token, she chooses not to submit to the petty demands of an impotent household tyrant when to do so is to violate her personhood.

In Elinor however, we see the response of individual autonomy to the inhibiting and fettering customs dictating female behavior. Thoroughly independent, Elinor has "a solid goodness of heart, that compensated for the occasional roughness, and habitual strangeness of her manners" (1:160, 161). We do not wish to argue with Elinor's agenda but rather with her method for achieving it. She is frank, sarcastic, aiming "rather to strike than to please, to startle than to conquer," and "prone to devote herself to whatever is new, wild or uncommon." Of herself she says, "I am fixed to cast wholly aside, the dainty common barriers, which shut out from female practice all that is elevated, or even natural" (1:356). She does not realize that one cannot escape the past simply by denying it. Of Juliet's propriety and reserve, which she interprets as raw calculation, she says, "You, Ellis, [are one] who never utter[s] a word of which you have not weighed the consequence; never indulge[s] a wish of which you have not canvassed the effects: who listen[s] to no generous feeling; who shrink[s] from every liberal impulse" (4:56).

Elinor's insightful speeches about patriarchal constraints and abuses engage our sympathy, but her actions do not. Her thought-lessness often places Juliet in difficult situations, as when she demands Juliet's collusion and secrecy in her schemes. Her revolutionary ideas are based on a shift in the understanding of human nature and culture that arises from the French Revolution. Rousseau's *âme déchirée* rebels against reason; its introspection tears the soul into two in conflict, not dialogue. This is a truth that cannot prevail outside ego consciousness; carried into the realm of public affairs, this notion survives as the myth of the self-made wo(man) who sees freedom in terms of personal civil liberties alone.[22] Her attempts simply to erase socially engendered roles and to create a society in which difference is nonexistent do not come to fruition; rather they alienate her from those she loves. Her purposive actions provoke corresponding reactions that defeat her goals.

Elinor, hopelessly in love with Harleigh, unsuccessfully attempts suicide in several public and dramatic scenes proving her despair and her love. Far from having the calculated effect, as though one could ever know the consequences of any act, her carefully orchestrated self-murder only serves to alienate her from Harleigh, while throwing Juliet and him together. Elinor is driven to a nearly mad pursuit of them, spying, questioning, harassing them at every turn. Harleigh sadly concludes that Elinor is governed by impulse, that she utters all that occurs to an imagination inflamed by passion and a wild courage that banishes restraint.

Like the revolutionary sentiment popular at the time, Elinor, "adept at turning the world upside down," as a "champion of her sex" espouses the rights of women and chafes at all restraint. Burney wrote to her father in 1792 that revolutionary sentiment gave "encouragement" to "political adventurers" who could "stimulate" people to "what they please." She goes on to describe the difference between historical and ahistorical action. The ahistorical act would expunge "all past experience, for the purpose of treating the world as if it were created yesterday, & every man, woman & Child, were let loose to act from their immediate suggestion, without reference to what is past, or sympathy in any thing that is present, or precaution for whatever is to come."[23] Like Robespierre and other great revolutionaries, Elinor wishes nothing more passionately than to initiate a new order of things. But like others in this novel, Elinor is bent more on her passions than she is bent upon responsive change. Sir Jasper says in particular terms about Elinor: "She seems to me . . . quite as well as it is possible for a person to be, who is afflicted with the restless malady of struggling for occasion to exhibit character; instead of leaving its display to the jumble of nature and of accident" (4:166). "The restless malady of struggling for occasion to exhibit character" recalls Burney's critical response to those ego-centered characters who display themselves in her diary. In contrast, "the jumble of nature and of accident" recalls Burney's voluminous journals, the "strange medley" out of which she discovers a self that is not a solitary individual. Elinor assumes herself to be a boundless original, a point of origin from which she authors herself and a new order. Her search for motives, her demand that everybody display his or her innermost desire transforms all agents into hypocrites. Her motives remain opaque to introspection and are hidden not only from others but most of the time from herself as well.

It is apparent in the course of the novel that Elinor is indeed a slave to passion and at points as hysteric in her discourse as Cecilia and Camilla are. Her "ruling passion" causes her to try to secure her identity in life-threatening scenes of great drama that focus attention upon her. She erroneously thinks that because women have been fettered in their thinking and barred from the authority to say, that the power to utter her every thought will liberate her.

Insofar as Elinor discloses herself even from within her attempts at autonomy, she partakes of the revelatory character of action. But she is not the author of her story as such, since her story is not a product that she can fabricate. Her staged acts reveal someone, but not necessarily the someone she thinks she is. Nevertheless, when things go wrong, she does reflect that she is "lost to my own definition of pride, of shame, of heroism" (4:58), and candidly admits to the isolating danger of autonomy when she says to Harleigh, "You could have corrected my errours [sic]; you, by your ascendance over my feelings, might have refined them into virtues" (1:418). Some may even argue that she represents a version of Wollstonecraft; if so, she is more a perversion, for Wollstonecraft herself argues against Rousseau's antinomy of nature-culture which isolates feelings from reason.[24] Moreover, even in her excesses, Elinor's courage is unforgettable and her appeal for female equality eloquent.

In contrast, Juliet's nonacting acting is not an ethical norm to be applied to everyone, to Elinor, for example, but is only ethical in the sense of being true to herself. When the evil official has determined Juliet's destiny by threatening the lives of those she loves, she acts to make herself the subject of *her* destiny. This does not change that destiny, but it changes how she relates to it. She shows us, furthermore, that her action is not a question of good or evil, an extrinsically imposed right or wrong ("whether or not it binds me to him"). The usual patriarchal point of view often casts her action in a light that makes it difficult to recognize as strength; nonetheless, Juliet's act says that she cannot be alienated from her tradition or herself, whatever that self may come to represent.

It is only the provisional predictability of past ties that lends Juliet an identity. When she fulfills her promise by saying, "I cannot tell my name," she also tests the viability of promise itself in the wilderness of the future. Namelessness and all the attendant uncertainties that flow from it make Juliet especially sensitive and responsive to unpredictability.

The impossibility for an unprotected female to be mistress of what she does is the price Juliet pays for her freedom to act spontaneously. Nonetheless, she realizes that even the most honored of traditions can be superseded by a spontaneous response. She cries, "Ought I . . . to submit to treatment so mortifying? Are there no boundaries to the exactions of prudence upon feeling? or, rather, is there not a mental necessity, a call of character, a cry of propriety, that should supersede, occasionally, all prudential considerations, however urgent?" (3:313). When she *must* choose between being true to her own personal integrity, a gathering of her entire past coming to bear upon the moment, or obeying a command that denies a past she has made part of herself, she responds truly—with spirit, dignity, and instinct.

For nearly five volumes Juliet flees her pursuer and suffers every kind of vicissitude in order to elude him, but when he finally catches up to her she no longer resists him. Miraculously, all the skeins of mystery are unraveled: the French official is killed, Juliet's foster family is freed, she is united with Harleigh and acknowledged by the Granvilles in name and with full inheritance. Harleigh eloquently explains that this strange turn of destiny is owed to the totally unpredictable but formative event of the French Revolution itself, which has "wonderfully" shaped the fate and fortune of those who have responded to it "according to their temperaments and dispositions." In this respect, "Revolution" is paradigmatic of all unexpected and initiating events. It is paradigmatic of what is never reducible to its antecedents as facts or causes of history. What Harleigh speaks of, even when couching his speech in clichés, is always poised at the brink of indeterminacy. This happening is the "infinite improbability" that forms not only the texture of event but also "in the school of refining adversity . . . in the trials, perils, and

hardships of a struggling existence" (5:386)—Juliet herself. It is in
the crucible of the patriarchal tradition that an Incognita shapes
herself and is shaped, and, to that extent, the happy ending is all
too predictable. Nonetheless, it is the infinitely improbable that generates that ending, not the specific aim-directed act of a particular
agent, not even when that agent takes the shape of the ideology of
will.

The infinitely improbable event discontinuous with a linear, historical past describes the truly historical event of naming. In observing a character who is named the nameless and who can never
take name for granted, we are made alive to the power of language
to reveal as it is never practiced in representation. We learn through
Juliet that to name according to the representational model says less.
By yielding to an unpredictable destiny, Juliet awakens to the power
of name. Sir Jasper, long Juliet's admirer, invokes this power when
he calls her "indefinable, unconquerable, unfathomable Incognita!"
(4:163). When her story, the untold story of the conceptualized female, is put into a narrative that participates in the public realm—
even a realm of "magistrates" and "censors"—the private "unsayable," once excluded from the public community, speaks. As Isak
Dinesen says, "All sorrows can be borne if you put them in a story
or tell a story about them." Burney tells a woman's story; we understand her suffering, appropriate her experience as our own, and
so she is "named."

5

'Nobody' Is the Author

Why, permit me to ask, must a female *be made Nobody? Ah! my dear, what were this world good for,* were *Nobody a female?*

—Fanny Burney

"INDEFINABLE, UNCONQUERABLE, UNFATHOMABLE" —these words apply to Burney the diarist as well as to Incognita the wanderer. Why a female must be made Nobody is a question that Burney raises in each of her novels. To be designated (made) nobody—a person of no importance or influence reified into an object like a container holding nothing—is the very notion of Nobody in its most pernicious sense. As one of the first of the recognized eigthteenth-century female "somebodies," Fanny Burney's "Nobody" not only had to cope with the paradox implied by the categories author *and* female, but with the then ascendant notion of the authority of the author as one who originates what is said. And yet, it is intriguing to observe that time and again in her diaries and prefaces, she renounced her authority and labeled herself "Nobody."[1] The playfulness of the address aside, the question needs to be asked, does gender condition the conception of oneself as a nonperson? The answer Burney gives to herself is really another question: "What were this world good for, *were* Nobody a female?" The play of meanings implied in that question exemplifies the Nobody we wish to ponder.

Burney's question emphasizes what for so long has been commonly assumed that it seems ridiculously self-evident. As minus-male, "woman" (O.E., wif-man) refers to the negative space of patriarchally engendered categories. The concept *Woman* derives from the practice of the culture that authors her by excluding her from

normative Man and masking her as "Incognita." The authority of
that long accepted "author" is today under question, as when Foucault observes that there was a time when narratives were "accepted,
circulated, and valorized without any question about the identity of
their author."[2] What then were we, and what now are we, to understand by author? When we rethink our notion of author less in
terms of "authority" and more in terms of "plurality," we are coming
closer in thought to Burney's "Nobody."

Rethinking the autonomous author in terms of an intersubjectivity
replaces the notion of an author as an individual "somebody" who
is outside and precedes a text with that of the "author function," a
multivoiced community that constitutes discourse. It is in much the
same idiom that Hannah Arendt observes:

> Although everybody started his life by inserting himself into the
> human world through action and speech, *nobody* is the author or
> producer of his own life story. In other words, the stories, the
> results of action and speech, reveal an agent but this agent is not
> an author. Somebody began it and is its subject in the twofold
> sense of the word, namely, its actor and sufferer, but *nobody* is its
> author. (*HC*, 184; emphasis added)

A glance into Burney's earliest diary, where "nobody is its author,"
will focus on those areas that deal with woman, the problem of
woman's writing, the patriarchal notion of author, and the concept
of author reinterpreted as plurality.[3] Where others concern themselves with either Burney the author or her portrait of an age, and
study both amply and well, this discussion focuses upon "Nobody"—
neither author nor authority. We will trace the apparently contradictory notion of Nobody, woman *and* author, in four ways: first, as
both sender of the message in her diary and its addressee; second,
as the pluralistic, multivoiced diarist: sender-addressee-community;
third, as the reified (patriarchal) author; and, fourth, as the renovated
author(s).

In the Berg Collection of the New York Public Library is a much
mutilated and penciled-over manuscript placed inside a faded blue
folder. Protected now from time and human hands, this is the earliest
(1768) of Fanny Burney's diaries.[4] It is addressed to a "Certain Miss
Nobody" and, crossed with three vertical lines, it is superscribed

with the following: "This strange medley of Thoughts & Facts was written at the age of 15. for my genuine & most private amusement. 'Fanny Burney.'" The nearly indecipherable condition of the manuscript and the huge editorial problem of the Burney correspondence—the editin by various members of the family, the sections cut out, rewritten, verwritten, burned, even the mass of material itself—is a testimony to the way in which diaries, letters, and journals do not fit our tidy notions of chronology, plot, or self-contained work produced by a particular somebody.

The idea of shaping a life from the strange medley of thoughts and facts that is available to one is decidedly *not* the same as assuming that self is already an identity and declared as such. Women write diaries because their individuality is neither the discovery of something already there nor the discovery of a truth hidden under what is there. As in the case of Evelina's diary, writing does not externally represent an inner state but discovers a for(u)m for thought. No one can know how the significance of one moment will bear on the next until the diary, the life, and the narrative are complete. Unlike a novel, the diary resists the very consistency of character and ordering of plot that it, as a record of a real person in historical time, purports to follow. Burney speaks of this consistent inconsistency of the person depicted in her diary:

> How truly does this Journal contain my real & undisguised thoughts—I always write in it according to the humour I am in, & if any stranger was to think it worth reading, how capricious—[inconsistent] & whimsical I must appear—one moment flighty & half mad,—the next sad & melancholy. No matter! it's truth & simplicity are it's [*sic*] sole recommendations. (1:61 [1769])[5]

Though "capricious" and "whimsical" appropriately describe the episodic nature of diary writing, they refer as well to a once commonplace notion of feminine identity. It is no accident that Burney adopts a written form compatible with a culturally preconceived female "form"; nonetheless, the diary in its secretive ("for my genuine and most private amusement") character allows for "undisguised thoughts" and frees ("according to the humour I am in") the diarist from the consistencies that a formal plot demands. Only a "stranger"—an outsider, for example those "GENTLEMEN" and "magistrates of the press, and Censors for the public" addressed in Burney's prefaces would demand consistency, judge the entries as "whimsical" and the diarist "flighty & half-mad." Addressed to Nobody, no one in authority, Burney's diary need not follow a pre-authorized form except that which the company of her thinking gives it. Instead, the diary gives to us Nobody in the form of a question left open to disovery.

Since there is some evidence that Burney wrote the superscription ("This strange medley of Thoughts & Facts") years later, and since the *Diary* re-collects letters to and from "Fanny," other journals, miscellaneous scraps of paper, and even her early fictional essays, the distinction of author as originating source is already an open question. And indeed since we, like Burney, are plunged *in medias res* into a "strange medley," that is to say, worlds and characters, the notion of a single work, let alone a single author, seems more convenient than actual. Whose authority could we accept anyway: the "Fanny" who wrote at age fifteen, the "Frances d'Arblay" who many years later edited the works and recollected the authoring of *Evelina* at an earlier age, or family members, friends, and literary scholars who edited the editing? All of them inscribed and reinscribed the work. The question might also be asked why we need to have an authority at all; but to think that problem through requires a preparation that is yet to be made. What is available to ponder is that if the "singularity" of the sender of the message is already called into question, what are we to say of the identity of the person to whom it is addressed?

Since the playful address to "A Certain Miss Nobody" remained a favorite form for Burney, her first diary entry bears closer examination:

> To have some account of my thoughts, manners, acquaintance & actions, when the Hour arrives in which time is more nimble than memory, is the reason that induces me to keep a Journal: a Journal in which I must confess my *every* thought, must open my whole Heart! But a thing of this kind ought to be addressed to some-body—(1:1 [1768])

Her impetus to write at all is "to have some account," that is, to make sense out of the "thoughts, manners, acquaintance & actions" that present themselves to her. More than transcribing historical facts, Burney writes in order to collect and recollect the jumbled assortment of "Thoughts & Facts" and account for them. She seems to take as her own precept Johnson's famous admonition to Boswell to write down everything while the impression is fresh and reserve judgment for later. Creating meaning from the strange medley is Burney's lifelong, never-to-be-completed project and the focus of her attention.

Of her undertaking Burney says that "a thing of this kind ought to be addressed to somebody." She then specifies who the somebody is that she converses with:

> I must imagion [*sic*] myself to be talking—talking to the most intimate of friends—to one in whom I should take delight in confiding, & remorse in concealment:—but who must this friend be? . . .
>
> To Nobody, then, will I write my Journal! since to Nobody can I be wholly unreserved—to Nobody can I reveal every thought, every wish of my Heart, with the most unlimited confidence, the most unremitting sincerity to the end of my Life! (1:1, 2 [1769])

If we presuppose Nobody to be in some way negative—a not-male, a not-Fanny, or a non-person—then we must replace Burney's own "delight in confiding" with "remorse in concealment": Burney's intimacy becomes alienation and Nobody becomes negation. What is worse, we fragment the plurality of Somebody-Nobody into two selves; one positive, one negative. Clearly the playful and affectionate relatedness between Fanny-Nobody in no way arises from the nay-saying of negation. Like Juliet, Burney cheerfully affirms Nobody as an open possibility.

This is the imaginative possibility of Nobody: "the most intimate of friends," somebody to confide in, somebody even to conceal things from, somebody—Nobody. She plays imaginatively the role of the other; the other not as outside, an alien, an authoritatively different other, but one who elicits intimacy, "unlimited confidence," and "unremitting sincerity." Intimacy and delight are shared by the two-in-one of thought, thinking as a form of friendship. By understanding otherness as *with*, not *outside* herself (as in the objectifying activity of the subject as *cogito*), she can assimilate difference, Nobody, unto

herself. In understanding otherness, she gives us a diary ostensibly
about herself which turns out to be possibility itself.

The imagined addressee as Nobody is also a plurality, not simply
another not-herself, that is, a nobody. Furthermore, Nobody is not
an object or identity, but a question the diarist asks of herself. The
diary is addressed to a self that is not "I" as *cogito,* but a no one
that is no "one."

> For what chance, what accident can end my connections with
> Nobody? No secret *can* I conceal from No-body, and to No-body
> can I be *ever* unreserved. Disagreement cannot stop our affection,
> Time itself has no power to end our friendship. The love, the
> esteem I entertain for Nobody, No-body's self has not power to
> destroy. From Nobody I have nothing to fear. (1:2 [1768])

Calling the principle of otherness implied in plurality "a friend"
signifies the intimacy and harmony of the relationship (her "connections") between the diarist and the other. In the world of patriarchal censorship she may have much to fear, but not from her friend
Nobody. All of these somebodies are distinguished by a relatedness
through difference that creates the so-called identity of the diarist
as a "self." Though all of these possibilities are Nobody and yet
somehow the "I," "No-body's self" and "Fanny"—all can be un-
reservedly, unfearfully distinct as well. There cannot be a self singular, but "selves" plural, not autonomy (named by herself) but
heteronomy (named by the other). As Luce Irigaray says,

> 'She' is indefinitely other in herself. This is doubtless why she is
> said to be whimsical, incomprehensible, agitated, capricious . . .
> not to mention her language, in which 'she' sets off in all directions
> leaving 'him' unable to discern the coherence of any meaning.
> Hers are contradictory words, somewhat mad from the standpoint
> of reason, inaudible for whoever listens to them with . . . a fully
> elaborated code in hand. (*TSNO,* 28–29; first ellipsis in text)

As for the concept *author,* whatever it may come to mean, Fanny-
Nobody already elides the distinction between self and other. The
loving reciprocity she shares with Nobody-as-other not even "Nobody's self"—here the diarist as a potential author-critic—has power

to destroy. How different this address is from the dedication to "the Authors of Monthly and Critical Reviews," "Inspectors," to whom she appeals with "temerity" for protection and "MERCY" from their resentment, scorn, disgust, and "contempt." How different too from an address to the "public" that she describes as craving "the penalty and forfeit of your bond," or possible "condemnation."

Burney directly connects "myself" with Nobody when she begins her diary of 1773: "I must therefore content myself with plainly & concisely proceeding with my Life and Opinions, addressed to My-self" (1:229). She continues her task of remembering events "which will otherwise Crowd so fast upon me,—that I shall not be able to recollect them. What a loss would that be! to my dear—Nobody!" (1:230). The loss would be, strictly speaking, to the addressee, to Nobody, as the community that would otherwise have no account of events. Time "crowds" this "community" not as an abstraction, chronology, measure; her verb suggests a congregation, a company of time "more nimble than memory" thronging and pressing, not plodding, sequential, factual.

Diaries are dangerous, tricky; they play games with time and memory: there is always the risk of discovery or theft, and there is the tendency of the diarist to "tell all" and risk censure—especially from the reading public and critics described above. Nobody is an appropriate name for a writer as self-effacing and as unprepared for fame as Burney. For all the humor implied in the address, writing a journal was not a task to be taken lightly. Burney's father cautioned her to take care of leaving her writings around the house. And in a conversation about her diary with a Miss Young, she records that "she says . . . it is the most dangerous employment young persons can have" (1:20 [1768]). Burney persists, saying, "I cannot see any harm in writing to *myself*" (1:20 [1768]). She continues to scribble, largely at night and in secret. Addressing Nobody, she says, "I write now from a pretty neat little Closet of *mine*. . . . Tell me, my dear, what Heroine ever yet existed without her own Closet?" (1:58 [1769]).

Were it not for Nobody rewritten as possibility in the diary, we would attribute a psychic lack to someone who named herself a nobody. It could also be argued that in a patriarchy all females are nobodies. We would even see in naming one's self "nobody" the inability to recognize personal differentiation or to assert individuality. At least we notice the diffidence of Nobody when she says in

1769, "I pass unnoticed—for so the world did by me" (1:90). Nonetheless, in turning from the playful addresses to Nobody and to the
diary's account of family, Burney finds little room within the confines
of her "closet" writing and domestic space for the authorized forms
the public exercises as "particularity": self-conscious introspection,
authority, and fame.

Although a diary invites a kind of self-absorbing introspection on
the part of the diarist, that is seldom the case for "Fanny." Individualism, what Burney calls "particularity," exemplifies the many
colorful and eccentric characters that she describes, but particularity
doesn't belong to someone who is negatively interpreted as "Nobody." Burney especially loved her sisters, Susan and Hetty, and
their feeling for her was reciprocal. But when she "worships" her
father, she falls down from friendly dialogue into abnegating de-
murral: "How strongly, how forcibly do I feel to whom I owe All
the happiness I enjoy!—it is to my Father! to this dearest, most
amiable, this best beloved—most worthy of men!" (1:61 [1769]). Actually, Burney felt that she had two fathers, her own, and her adopted
"Daddy" Crisp, with whom she much more freely shared her
thoughts, even though there is little evidence that Dr. Burney, whom
Fanny so feared to displease, was by any means a harsh authori-
tarian. Dr. Burney seems to have affection toward her, but as he
was busy and she one of many children, of a retiring mien and a
quiet, respectful attitude, he consistently underestimated her abili-
ties. There is much in her relation to her father to comment on,
but that must be deferred for a time.

Shy and painfully self-conscious when noticed in a social setting,
Burney the novelist will be reduced to terror after achieving public
notoriety. Yet in those earliest of journals, Burney has remarkably
little to say about herself. She is there of course, but only as a
necessary character among the combined household that forms her
father's family and that of his second wife. That family is the source
of the diarist's sense of herself and her world; she would later cut
out large sections of her journal for the sake of prudence and the
protection of her family's privacy. She decided, it seems, to avoid
one of the dangers of writing a diary by not telling "all." Of course
we have the many letters she wrote to others and they to her, but
hers are filled, and take great pains to be filled, with scenes, conversations, characters, and events that passed within the context of

the Burney household and society. By examining the diarist's account of an episode in which *she* is one of the central characters, we come to understand how writing gives Burney the individuality she can later re-create for Evelina.

The sensitivity to the social delicacy that so permeates the novels can be tracked through an account in which Burney's deepest feelings are at stake. Where so much emphasis is given to the amalgam of the private and the social, it is no wonder that marriage exemplifies the paradigmatic social relationship. As she so often does, Burney reveals her feelings about this subject through her observation of someone else:

> Had I been for my sins Born of the male Race, I should certainly have added one more to Miss Linley's Train. She is really beautiful. . . . With all this, her Carriage is modest & unassuming, & her Countenance indicates diffidence, & a strong desire of pleasing. . . .
>
> I think that so young a Woman, Gifted . . . who can preserve herself, unconscious of her charms & diffident of her powers,—has merit that entitles her to the strongest approbation, & I hope, to the greatest happiness:—a union from affection with a man who deserves her! (1:251 [1773])

When Dr. Marchmont warns Edgar in *Camilla* that "an establishment" is a single female's primary concern, he is not far from the understanding that appears in the diary. No wonder, then, that the one really painful and embarrassing situation for Burney in the early journals is when an obsequiously attentive Mr. Barlow proposes—twice. This episode not only captures the diarist's self-deprecating humor, Mr. Barlow's officious sentiment, Dr. Burney's motives, and the Fanny "character's" own awkwardness, but also shows us the pressure a woman is put under to "find an establishment." Most importantly of all, however, it shows us how the composite voice called Nobody, both sender and addressee, is also the community.

Since Burney does not love young Barlow, she will not consider marriage to him even though both fathers in her life—her own and Mr. Crisp—entreat her at least to give Barlow some consideration. Causing Fanny great pain, her father urges her not to immediately reject Barlow. His constraint forces her to appear either rude or trifling. Writing to Daddy Crisp, the diarist earnestly says that "the *heart* ought to be heard, and mine will never speak a word I am sure, for any one I do not truly enough honour to cheerfully, in all things serious, obey" (*ED,* 2:51 [1775]). Mr. Crisp begs "Fannikin" to remember this is not a marrying age without a fortune and to "consider the situation of an unprotected, unprovided woman." These voices of urgency representing the social view of marriage become part of the discussion that Nobody as addressee has with Burney the diarist.

In asserting that it is incumbent upon every female who refuses a man "to keep from the world his unsuccessful choice" (*ED,* 2:61 [1775]), we hear the code of the community in conflict with the heart of the diarist. The gushing young man implores Burney not to refuse him as marriage is "the social state one is meant for." Though she concurs with his view of social destiny, she refuses his proposal, but also adds, "—but you know there are many odd characters in the world—and I am one of them" (*ED,* 2:66 [1775]). The distinctive delicacy that seems so much a part of "Frances Burney" arises out of what we can see of the personal conviction in the diarist, the conflicting attitudes of the community, and the young Burney who is narrated. If her father still presses "an early establishment" upon her, she fears "the utter impossibility of resisting not merely my father's *persuasion,* but even his *advice*" (*ED,* 2:69 [1775]). Burney can seldom resist her father's advice, and later writes her novels with his approbation always in mind.

Clearly this episode demonstrates how Fanny Burney makes meaning out of this "strange medley of Thoughts & Facts" by writing about it. The more extensive significance of the passage is that it is one of the few occasions when she talks about herself—and yet, even here, it is less a self that speaks about itself than the multiple voices of a community. These voices of a community converge in the reflective detachment of the diarist within the space of writing. It is as though she is *nothing but* the place of convergence, and yet as nobody, nothing does not mean what she writes is absurd or meaningless. The "whimsical," strange and inconsistent, appears meaningless only from the point of view of patriarchal authority and its rules governing the logic of the written word. When she risks meaning nothing by becoming nobody, she begins to play with previously unthought and unarticulated possibilities. Derrida makes this same point when he says, "To risk meaning nothing is to start to play, and first to enter in the play of *différance* which prevents any word, any concept, any major enunciation from coming to summarize and to govern."[6]

Yet even the place of writing is not a solitary position, for Burney inhabits neither the writing nor the place of origin of an author outside the text. She *is* the community in that she reflects the community's attitude back upon the event of the proposal, the most social relationship in her world. The particular proposal, the authority of the social code, the disposition of the two male authorities in her life, the urgency with which she must decide, the sense of propriety that requires a quick response—all are reflected through the good humored understanding of her written perspective. In other words, Fanny Burney both speaks about the community and reflects community. She is neither an introspective, autonomous entity speaking in the confessional mode nor a ventriloquist adopting various voices, for either position would still make the author a singular entity. Yet she is not simply a copier transcribing events, for she accounts by rethinking, and hence, interpreting them.

If her sense of personhood comes from being with the community, her becoming consistent with herself gives the diaries and the Nobody we know from them their ethos and integrity. That well-being as being-with-the-world does not by any means preclude its sorrows and troubles:

> For my own part, I applaud & honour every Body who, having that lively & agonizing sensibility which is *tremblingly Alive* to each emotion of sorrow, can so far subdue the too exquisite refinement of their feelings as to permit themselves to be consoled in affliction. Why should Despair find entrance into the short Life of man? (1:157 [1771])

Certainly we know that Burney suffered during this time by having to cope with a hated stepmother, a second family, various family scandals, and an often obtuse father. Yet she can find consolation and solace in the reflective space of writing:

> Well—I *have* slept, & perhaps *have* reflected—but as the sleep came last, it has drove all reflections away which at all tended to the

detriment of this little Employment; & therefore, once more wel-
come my Pen! my Nobody! my dear faithful Journal!— (1:67
[1769])

The world already underway, that configuration of the social group
in the diary and its importance to the diarist can be misunderstood,
or worse, trivialized. The social is more than spending time with
others or practicing communal customs. The diary incorporates
"World" into the private world of the diarist just as becoming a
novelist will incorporate the private diarist into the larger horizon
beyond friends and family. The relationship of the diarist with Nobody shapes and is shaped by the intersubjectivity of Nobody and
the social world in which she moves. If that elides the boundary
between sender and addressee, what is to be said of the boundary
between sender and world?

Burney shares at least a common sense with her world; indeed,
the Nobody to whom she speaks is also the world. By common sense,
a now much less common meaning is implied. Arendt says that
common sense had once meant the "one by which all other senses,
with their intimately private sensations, were fitted into the common
world" (HC, 283). The opposite is the Cartesian sense of the term
where persons have in common, not the world, but the structure
of their minds.[7] Having only self-consciousness in common, the
Cartesian tends to be alienated not only from the world but from
others. Burney's diary vividly contrasts the confessional mode of
speech, that form of private introspection that the bourgeois and
Protestant turned into a sincerity or intimacy that self-validates,
ensuring that one is free, truthful, and above reproach. In writing
about the Barlow episode, "Fanny" affirms her self-respect precisely
because she so seldom focuses on self. In other words, Burney's
common sense fits her private sensations to that of the community
rather than forcing the world to fit the contours of her feelings.

Burney's openness, a blend of concern and detachment shapes
"the sly rogue's" satirical bent and her common sense. Speaking as
the community enabled the diarist to observe herself dispassionately
in the proposal episode. As an intimate observer—Johnson called
her a "character-monger"—she neither lets subtle distinctions in
mood and behavior escape her nor lets the solipsistic play of the
mind with itself concern her:

I have been wavering in my mind whether I should ever again touch this Journal, unless it were to commit it to the Flames—for this same *mind* of mine, would fain persuade me that this same *Journal* of mine is a very ridiculous—trifling & useless affair; & as such, would wisely advise me to part with it for ever—but I felt at the same Time, a regret, a loss of something in forbearing to *here unburthen* myself—the pleasure which (in imagination at least) awaits me in the perusal of these sheets hereafter, pleaded strongly in favour of continuing to encrease them. (1:70 [1769])

Because of her intimate bonding with community, Burney lacks the detached, bitter irony of other satirists, but not the bemused sense of the satirical. The diaries are often scintillating and charming, especially in capturing the nuances of conversation and character. This fittedness of the individual and community or *sensus communis* permeates Burney's writing. She doesn't write from outside the community, as the ironic observer so often does, and affirm her wit by ironizing all. She chides herself for hasty judgment:

I have quite forgot the wise resolution I so often make of never Judging of people by first sight!—Pity! that we have all the power of *making* resolutions so readily, & so properly, & that few or none are capable of *keeping* them!—but here again am I Judging of other's fortitude by my own weakness!—O dear, I am always to be wrong? (1:63 [1769])

Notice how in dialogue with the two-in-one of thought she modifies her first observation:

However, I think I may prevail on myself not to be my *own* Judge too rashly—why should I think I am *always* to be wrong?—I know not I am sure; certain it is I have hitherto never been otherwise; but *that* ought not to discourage me, since so inconsistent is Human nature allow'd to be, that for that very reason 'tis impossible I should be the same Creature at the conclusion as at the beginning of my life. (1:63 [1769])

This example shows how her perception of herself refracts the experience of diarist-community. Her writing flows from within the community, flows between the observance of appearance and habit, between the individuating character of her speech and her dialogical relationship to others, between the community and the "Creature" who finds it "impossible" to be the same "at the conclusion as at the beginning" of her life. The passage is extraordinary in that it shows not only the contradictory impulses within her but also her sense of the inconsistencies in Human nature—a nature deemed permanent and stable in some accounts of eighteenth-century thought. In fact, so much does she feel her person to be inextricable from the community that she would much later remark to a friend upon her marriage to General D'Arblay: "Domestic comfort and social affection have invariably been the sole as well as ultimate objects of my choice." Her writing does not pit her against the world, since world for her is a space of "domestic comfort and social affection."

Not only does Burney live in the first modern society, she also is keenly aware of its demand upon her allegiance. Custom, decorum, delicacy—these are more than labels and signify more than a prudish and unquestioning attitude toward the normative. Notwithstanding her laments against custom, Burney also observes how being "particular" can be liberating. Nonetheless, she is well aware of the cost of such particularity. She observes too many who, "being particular," pay little regard to the custom of the world by indulging in raillery and disdain.

It can be argued that an individual's particularity, striving, like Elinor in *The Wanderer*, to be someone by asserting one's self over against the world, is an authority of self-command not available to one relegated by culture to the position of nobody. But this form of egocentrism is gained not only at the expense of others but at the expense of the person as well. That is, particularity is a cost not just *to* a person but *of* the person—since only being-within-the-world lends one any particularity at all.

Burney writes about a comment from her father to someone who mistook her for her sister Hetty: "You may have observed, my Lord, that People who Live together, naturally catch the looks & air of one another, & without having one Feature alike, they contract a *something* in the whole Countenance which strikes one as a resemblance" (1:69 [1769]). She recognizes intersubjectivity when she records that "people who live together" "contract," that is, draw together, enter into an agreement, catch the "something in the whole," the individuality in relationship to others which lends them distinction.

A composite Fanny Burney is no one in the sense that she lacks a unitary identity; Nobody is a question she asks in dialogue with herself where the I is both the one who asks and the one who answers. She later writes to this composite "myself": "I shall reserve all my forces for those by way of *amende honorable*—to—whom?—why to myself, that is to Nobody! Heigh-ho! poor me! Are Nobody and I one and the same person?" (*ED,* 1:338 [1774]). Burney is kept from slipping into Nobody as negation, as "one and the same person," by the openness of her question.

The ego inherent in the usual patriarchal understanding of the individual as one who spins a world out of "*his*" own conciousness depends upon this prior condition of Nobody as possibility. "Nobody" functions as that prior condition. "*Her*" sense of self comes from being within the world, even that patriarchal world which generates the diaries, and gives us the Nobody we know from them their ethos and integrity.

What gradually emerges, then, from Burney's diary is neither a sacrifice of personhood to the social, as though Nobody were nothing at all, nor a means for subsuming all to the structure of one's own mind, as though world were nothing at all. The patriarchal author who originates creative genius in the mind fabricates a text as a sort of museum of completed events. What is remarkable in Fanny Burney's journal instead is a nonoriginative, ongoing process of reflective dialectic. That is, if she does not write, it is often because her thinking is busily attending to others, as when she once again addresses Nobody: "I have not written this age—& the reason is, my thoughts have been all drawn away from myself & given up to my dear Hetty" (1:139 [1770]). She freely gives up her "thoughts" and lets them be "drawn away" from herself and to "dear Hetty." She shows us how identity functions intersubjectively, slipping in-between the "I" who has not written, the "thoughts" drawn away from "myself," the community of Hetty and Fanny together, and finally the addressee, Nobody. Thus, in tracking the diarist first as Nobody and second as community, we discover that sender, addressee, and community all function as author: the "I" who writes and at the same time is "written" into the writing, the author Fanny Burney

supposedly outside it (also "I"), and of course Nobody ("friend,"
"myself," and "Fanny" within the writing).

We're now in a position to trace the relationship between an
author who is Nobody, an author-function ("Fanny Burney"), and
a patriarchal, or representational, author. We have already seen in
the novels and diary how character is individuated not by "particularity," nor by introspection, but by the community. Burney's well-
being depends upon a rich texture of communal relationships in
which the boundary between self and others is fluid, intimate, reciprocal, neither inside nor outside. In wrenching contrast, her extraordinary regard for her father—"Author of my being," and
elsewhere, one "to whom I owe all the earthly happiness I enjoy"—
differs dramatically from the being-with character of Fanny Burney.
Often her journal entries erupt in an outburst of praise for her
father's "every virtue." What is peculiar here is that her regard for
Dr. Burney is a disposition toward an absolutely separated, outside
other. When in the dedication to *Evelina* she refers reverentially to
him as "Author of my being," the nuance of the term "Author" is
both patriarchal and theological. When she sees him as father-god,
she defines herself as the traditional female, taking upon herself the
burdensome dilemma of Woman as concept that the diaries otherwise
dismantle. "Fannikin" reifies and valorizes her father as absolute
other by removing him from the community—outside the play of
the world and, in principle, beyond reach. Practically, he is removed
from the processes of community, and his judgment denied to her
critical scrutiny. At times she makes herself an unthinking slave to
this idolatry of the father, an activity that reduces her own possible
personhood and determines the patriarchal concept of woman. This
reductionism is demonstrated in several episodes.

It is during the most miserable time of Burney's life when, as a
spinster lady-in-waiting, actually keeper of the robes, at the court
of King George III and Queen Charlotte, the deferential relationship
of a near-fortyish woman to her father achieves tragic pathos. Having, by the wish of her father, accepted this prestigious position at
court—one that nearly amounts to being a slave for life—Burney
quickly discovers how ill-suited she is to the task. There she enlists
others to beg her father for approval to resign from the court, a
resignation that, because of her father's respect for royalty, Burney's
fear, and the prerogative of the queen, takes nearly two years to

conclude. During those five long years at court, Burney makes promises to herself in an attempt to resolve her inner turmoil: "I now
took the most vigorous resolutions to observe the promise I had made
my dear father. . . . Oh! could they look within me. I am *married,*
my dearest Susan—I look upon it in that light. . . . What then now
remains but to make the best wife in my power? I am bound to it
in duty, and I will strain every nerve to succeed."[8]

At odds with herself, caught among her father's wishes, her duty
to the queen, her own misery, and worst of all, cut off from others,
Burney's resolution fails her. No longer friends with herself, well-
being disrupted, she becomes her own adversary. Nonetheless, her
deep unhappiness and even the poor health resulting from it are a
tribute to her earlier strength in adversity.

Burney seems to constrain herself from questioning her great
esteem for her father, in spite of his interference with her writing
in the form of advice or pressure. Dr. Burney certainly felt no
constraint in dictating his advice. He was extremely proud of her
efforts—almost blindly so—though he tended to fret over public
reception of her work. In her relationship to him, so paradigmatic
of the best and worst sides of the patriarchy, she assumes the traditional female role that is consistent with her cultural understanding
of herself as woman. That understanding is inconsistent with the
plurality available to us through her intimate friendships, her gaiety,
spirit of satire, keenly intelligent observation of people—that world
in communion with herself—which informs her diary and novels at
their best. In comparison to the early Nobody entries, the court
years (1786–1791) chart the struggling dialogue of one not in harmony
with oneself, of one who feels isolated and painfully aware of her
difference as nobody.

In a patriarchal culture where the authoritative discourse designates "not male" as "nobody," and where nobody is powerless and,
in effect, voiceless—to be designated woman is, literally, to be nobody. This sense of nobody, vastly reductive of the plurality of the
diarist's Nobody, is one that Fanny seems to yield to when she defers
to her father as author of, and authority over, her being. Not only
can we track the reified concept *woman* through the "discourse of
the father," then, but also through the patriarchal notion of authority.

As difficult as the later court years were on both Burney and her
productivity as a writer, the heavier burden by far was the patriarchal

authority inherent in her fame as an author, for fame is largely a phenomenon of the centered author. It is far from trivial that Burney's fame coincides historically with the notion that writing originates a text over which the author as a "rational entity" can, and even must, exercise rights of property.[9] One of those property rights is the fame by which the world disowns its own voice in the work and relegates the author to the position of the father outside community. When Burney tells Mr. Crisp her writing is only "trifling stuff," there is more than modesty in the phrase. The world encourages her to reinterpret "trifling" as "originating," and from that moment, she must bear the burden of "genius." Mr. Crisp replies to her, "You cannot but know *that trifling, that negligence, that even incorrectness*, now and then in familiar epistolary writing, is the very soul of genius" (*ED*, 2:41 [1775]).

When in 1777 Burney divulges the secret of her scribbling "trash" to her father, he does not object to "my having my own way in total secrecy and silence to all the world" (*FMB*, 73 [1777]). But when the book is published and a small circle discovers the author not to be, as was commonly thought, a man, but literally, a nobody, Burney records her response to becoming a public somebody:

> I have an exceeding odd sensation, when I consider that it is now in the power of *any* and *every* body to read what I so carefully hoarded even from my best friends ... a work ... lodged, in all privacy in my bureau, may now be seen by every butcher, and baker ... throughout the three kingdoms. (*ED*, 2:214 [1778])

The public has now become the "stranger" alluded to earlier, that abstracted, distanced community of "Investigators" not acquainted with the diarist.

After the initial success of *Evelina*, when Burney first meets Mrs. Thrale at Streatham, she faces a severe test from a Mr. Lort who refers to *Evelina* disparagingly in her presence. Not for the first time, Burney runs from the room—and fame—in embarrassment. Later Mrs. Thrale laughingly warns her in private: "So you thought just to have played and sported with your sisters and cousins, and had it all your own way; but now you are in for it! But if you will be an author and a wit, you must take the consequences!"(*FMB*, 93 [1778]). Those "consequences" turn the paradox of the woman author into a lived contradiction, for authorship belongs to the legal and institutional structure of patriarchy that circumscribes, determines, and articulates the reaches of discourse (Foucault, 130). In other words, the notion of author as sovereign creator of his discourse is patriarchal in a sense far broader than gender: it is a version of individualism that radically misunderstands the process of writing itself. That Burney reflects and accepts the female role of her culture there can be little doubt. She declared in 1779: "I would a thousand times rather forfeit my character as a writer, than risk ridicule or censure as a female. I have never set my heart on fame, and therefore would not, if I could, purchase it at the expense of all my own ideas of propriety" (*FMB*, 103). Since propriety is a female role conceived by the patriarchy as passive, even voiceless, a woman has no access to, no authority over, those systems that try to determine the reaches of discourse. Comfort with the code of the patriarchy both frees and binds "Fanny Burney" to it; writing as nobody dissolves that double bind.

For a woman to write as an author, that is, actively to participate in the system of valorization based on a need to establish authenticity or attribution, is tantamount to exceeding the limits of her role as female. Authenticity and attribution are available only to the father and the discourse of the father. The notion of author as creator, sovereign over his text, is implicitly denied to woman as the second term in a pair of dichotomies that gives sovereignty to man. Though Nobody *functions* as an author, she cannot *be* an author or authority in the patriarchal sense.

Burney's experience with fame is outside her play with possibility in the early diary. A woman and recognized Author fragments the corporate person and (mis)represents herself. Since Nobody as a possibility and the individual entity "Fanny Burney" are incongruous, she cannot follow the advice of Dr. Johnson and "learn to be a swaggerer," a distinction she has earned, not courted.[10]

From the doubts expressed by Burney and her two fathers about her authority as an author, one gets a sense that the popular notion of author as "magistrate," legislator and critic, is antithetical to the delimitation of woman. Even after a gratifying public reception of *Evelina* in 1778, Burney writes: "What my daddy Crisp says, 'that it would be the best policy, but for pecuniary advantages, for me to write no more,' is exactly what I have always thought since *Evelina* was published" (*FMB*, III [1778]). She alludes to the problem of authority in a letter written to her sister Susan about her second published work:

> The wisest course I could take, would be to bid an eternal adieu to writing; then would the cry be, "'Tis pity she does not go on!—she might do something better by and by,"... but would a future attempt be treated with the same mercy?... Those who have met with less indulgence would all peck at any second work; and even those who most encouraged the first offspring might prove enemies to the second, by receiving it with expectations which it could not answer. (*FMB*, 81 [1778])

The new audience is no longer just the plurality of the early diaries; the public has constituted itself as authority, like the reified father, violating its own pluralism in presuming to speak as "the rooster preceding the egg" and "peck" at her second offspring.

The intrusive standard from outside her own intimate process seems to Burney like an audience of so many hostile fathers. While so discomfited, she does acquire a craft, learns her role as writer, and finds a place in the broader community of her readers. Nonetheless, when she is inhibited by the conception of the authority that validates written texts, she retreats from autonomous author and reinhabits her plurality; she keeps on writing and keeps the conversation going.

After the turn of the century and when she is "the famous Miss Burney," her journal often contains entries written years earlier. She sometimes loses sight of herself as audience when she is forced to write for a living, to depend on her father to approve her efforts, and to enlist the authority of fame as a "known author" for remuneration. She withdraws from production her comedy "Love and Fashion" upon the wish of her father. Once again, she abases herself to her father-Author of her being:

> I am sure my dear father will not infer, from this appeal, I mean to parallel our works. No one more truly measures her own inferiority, which, with respect to yours, has always been my pride. I only mean to show, that if my muse loves a little variety, she has an hereditary claim to try it. (*FMB*, 271 [1800])

When Burney hypostatizes her father as she does above, and thereby reifies herself, she participates in the objectifying authority of the patriarchy. In overrating her father she underrates him and condemns him to the loneliness of community denied. The logic of patriarchy only leaves open to her either the idolatry or the rejection of the father. Yet Nobody has shown us that what both precedes and transcends the boundaries of isolated selves is the conversation of dialogue, the art of thinking that patriarchal authorship precludes. Paradoxically then, renouncing herself as entity by assuming the author functioning as Nobody, an open possibility, liberates her from the female identity that the patriarchy calls nobody, and Incognita triumphs.

After the 1814 publication of *The Wanderer* her task is to edit the voluminous materials of her father. Tired, yet obedient and devoted, she publishes in 1832 the memoirs of Dr. Burney. They are harshly judged and poorly received by those in authority.

Which brings us full circle to the Nobody first addressed in the juvenile diary. We have seen that the diarist is not an author writing to an audience of one, split into two, but that the *writing* is constitutive of Burney as she writes to "my dear, faithful, ever attentive Nobody" (1:97 [1770]). In these entries we hear neither one voice masked as many nor an isolated consciousness. Instead, Nobody–Burney as the author function is constitutive of the patriarchal subject and his notion of woman. Nobody–Burney gives rise to a variety of subjective possibilities that constitutes individuality.

Recall that when Burney writes her diary to Nobody, the audience she has in mind is a corporate self: "I will suppose you, then, to be my best friend; . . . my dearest companion—& a romantick Girl" (1:2 [1768]). Intersubjectivity, her being-with-others is constitutive both of the audience and the author. Nothing indicates more clearly that Burney exists in the plural than that solitude causes her to converse with herself in her diary, a lesson she will pass on to her heroine Evelina. It is in this awareness of herself with herself that thinking as conversation occurs. The plural woman Burney inscribes as human being and other is significant long before the voice of a female author ever speaks in the written word. As sender-addressee-community *and* woman—that is, the multiple possibilities of Nobody—she overcomes the patriarchal insistence that she is absolutely other and therefore nobody.

In 1771 the diarist writes, "Yes my dear Journal! yes! with the more pleasure shall I regard Thee, thou faithful preserver and repository of my Thoughts & Actions" (1:180 [1771]). Hence, Burney's friend is not only herself, not only her journal, but thinking itself. When she eschews introspection, she renounces not the reflection of her thought upon the state of her being but "the sheer cognitive concern of consciousness with its own content" (*HC*, 280). This sense of plurality, Burney both as a particular and as Nobody, exemplifies the process of thinking itself.

Thinking is the companion Burney keeps in all her writing. She so values this company that she strives to keep her in good repair. Thanks to being Nobody, Burney discovers for us that the author is a function and the reader a plurality, that there is no individual identity at either end of the text, for if there were, there would be no need of discourse at all—or rather the discourse would be silence. Beyond the notion of authority, both reader and author are shaped by the message, indeed, *are* the message. The message—an invitation that invites a reply—encompasses the dense web of relationships among sender, receiver, and community, and constantly re-creates it. Writing disseminates meaning, figuring and de-figuring bodies: somebody, nobody, author, and world. Where Burney and Nobody slide in between something and no-thing as they have in this discussion, dismantling and reconstructing both person and author, well might one ask again, as the final chapter of this study will, "What were this world good for, *were* Nobody a female?"

6

Woman's Revelation
and Women's Revolution

*"Cyclops, you ask me for my famous name. I will tell you . . . Nobody
is my name. My father and mother call me Nobody, as do all the others
who are my companions. . . . "*

*Then from inside the cave strong Polyphemos answered: "Good friends,
Nobody is killing me by force or treachery."*

—*The Odyssey*, Book IX

BURNEY'S DESCRIPTION of the wanderer as "unknown, unnamed,
without any sort of recommendation" (1:151) echoes the words that
she had applied to herself in the diaries and her original dedication
to *Evelina* about her own "entrance into the world" as an Incognita,
under concealment so to speak. "So affrighted" that "what she
scribbled, if seen, would but expose her to ridicule," Burney again
raises the issue of concealment in the *Memoirs of Dr. Burney* by referring to the pen as her greatest but also her "clandestine delight."
She recapitulates the story of *Evelina*'s authoring:

> That a work, voluntarily consigned by its humble author, even
> from its birth, to oblivion, should rise from her condemnation,
> and, 'Unpatronized, unaided, unknown,' make its way through
> the metropolis . . . whence, triumphantly, it should be conveyed to
> Sir Joshua Reynolds; made known to Mr. Burke; be mounted
> even to the notice of Dr. Johnson, and reach Streatham . . . and,—
> by mere chance,—in the presence of Dr. Burney; seemed more
> like a romance, even to the Doctor himself, than anything in the
> book that was the cause of these coincidences.[1]

Approval by the "Authors of the Monthly and Critical Reviews"
could ensure the truth claims of the artist. "Unpatronized, unaided,
unknown" becomes an inscription for all those female "scribblers"

who took up the pen in an attempt to write their own narrative destinies. In her original dedication to *Evelina* (written in the form of a letter) we can contrast the "trifling production" of one "without name, without recommendation, and unknown" to the "extensive plan" of the "Gentlemen" who observe and examine with absolute "impartiality." Nobody, "unpatronized, unaided, unowned," cannot claim such authorial privilege and power. Thus, Burney's own history and the histories of her earlier heroines culminate in "Incognita." Each story tells of a "Nobody" who faces a public world of strangers, those demanding consistency of plot and person. Each story drawn from the intersubjectivity of the diaries and journals, the "strange medley of Thoughts & Facts," "whimsical," "flighty & half-mad," narrates "Nobody" within the community of writing. The narrative revelation of woman's cry as Nobody articulates a potential voice for women's revolution.

So far, this study has explored the relationships among Evelina, Camilla, and Cecilia's hysteria or mode of forbidden speech (Nobody as a conceptual Woman of no account) and a certain pathology of cultural assumptions underlying the history of an individual identity, as explored in the eighteenth-century novel. Revealing the relationships among name, identity, and those conditions symptomatic of woman's hysteric discourse can clarify issues left unresolved until now. Though the point has been made in the earlier chapters that woman's "cry" (regardless of whatever that cry has come to mean) has much to say to us about writing, irrationality, and affectivity, it can say even more in the light of our discussion of namelessness in *The Wanderer*. That is, the "female difficulties" of Incognita, like the symptoms of woman's suffering brought on by representational discourse, take on secondary importance to the prevailing issue of namelessness, the female inheritance of Burney and her creations. If now we return to the earlier novels and re-examine them no longer in terms of woman's symptoms, but in terms of her search for a discourse that allows her to name, we may discover that *her* existential suffering and *our* imaginations may be redeemable by namelessness itself.

Namelessness is analogous to Evelina's unsettled social position resulting from the clouded circumstances obscuring her origin.[2] As the unacknowledged heir of her father and so unnamed, Evelina conceals her legitimate surname of "Belmont" and bears a borrowed name. Legitimacy incarnates patriarchal power, assuring its continuity. Female purity guards patrilineal succession and merits a right to name by marriage only; women become name-bearers only by bearing males.

Evelina's right to carry the patrilineal name is symptomatic of woman's lack of legitimate discourse. Her birthright cannot be subject to public or legal claim, for if it were, it would violate the rule of female propriety, damage her father's honor, and call her own legitimacy into question. She has no other recourse but to rely on others to intercede in her behalf, or else she risks in a public appeal censure of her father's name, and therefore, of her own.

Acquiring a name (paternal or marital recognition) will lend Evelina the authority to speak (name) in accordance with accepted standards and so identify her within the social realm. Evelina learns unhappily "how requisite are birth and fortune to the attainment of respect and civility" (276). That is, in a mercantile age, name acquires a material denomination by its ability to represent commercial value more than its ability to reveal human or intrinsic worth. Evelina, as Willoughby says, is a "girl of obscure birth, whose only dowry is her beauty, and who is evidently in a state of dependency," and for that reason he is opposed to an honorable connection with her. "Birth and fortune" or name (like money) become the instruments for representing and analyzing measurable, hence legitimate, value.

Social status, beauty, and wealth coined as the name that permits a person's worth to be representable can be circulated and exchanged like money. Foucault describes this phenomenon of the classical age in *The Order of Things*:

> All wealth is *coinable*; and it is by this means that it enters into *circulation*—in the same way that any natural being was *characterizable*, and could thereby find its place in a *taxonomy*; that any individual was *nameable* and could find its place in an *articulated language*; that any representation was *signifiable* and could find its place, in order to be *known* in a *system of identities and differences*. (175)

To enter the system of "identities and differences" manifested by a map of names means that the right or ability to ascribe a name is

an act of power and authority. To be silenced or represented as silent
in that system is to be a no-one, no-thing, that which cannot be
nameable nor given to naming. Foucault says, "In the classical age,
nothing is given that is not given to representation" (78; emphasis
added). Evelina's persistent belief in an essential innocence makes
her "characterizable"; her marriage makes her "nameable" so that
she can find her place in an "articulated language"; and, most
important, her writing letters makes her "signifiable," enabling her
to enter the system of identities and differences known as representation. Nevertheless, as we have already seen, "her pen acquires a
voice of its own."[3]

Evelina believes herself to be deprived of authority and so to need
the guidance of masculine intellect and the directive of patriarchal
will. Near the end of the novel when Evelina is soon to be married,
she writes to Villars: "It would be highly improper I should dispose
of myself forever so very near the time which must finally decide *by
whose authority* I ought to be guided" (352; emphasis added). And yet
long before the awaited event, Evelina demonstrates her own authority by authoring her journal-diary. It is one thing for Evelina
to acquire speech and a surname, however, and quite another to
write. Writing brings with it the attendant dangers of theft, loss,
misinterpretation, and most dangerous of all, the claim to a citizenship reserved exclusively for man and the written word—authority
over language in the "republic of letters."

Authority over language as a tool to command is a position that
neither Evelina nor Burney claims. Evelina's "entrance into the
world" marks not only her debut into society, but as an author
marks, that is to say, signifies, her entry into the world that constitutes the "republic of letters." For her, writing is an activity fraught
with dangers because she writes under a cultural prohibition barring
woman from the act of naming. Writing, then, is a politically pow-
erful act, a revolutionary event.

When Evelina asks what she shall be called, she is not only asking
what she shall be designated, but what will let show, let *be* her name.
Calling brings closer what it calls; it brings near to our attention
the previously unsaid. Naming does not arbitrarily impose titles like
a subject designating object; name gives thought, speech, language,
voice to human being. It is no wonder, then, that one of the perils

in a patriarchal culture for the woman who names, who writes, is to have her letter "purloined."

When Willoughby purloins the letter written by Evelina to Orville, his act seems to be a robbery of her authority as a subject, that is, of her authorial authority. But letters also enable the novel to appear without the controlling voice of an author. The author, now as editor, frees the heroine to narrate her own story, but even that telling has no final authority because both Evelina and Burney disavow that kind of controlling authorship. The letter is diverted, deferred from the normal path of its direction and is thus "a letter in sufferance." Woman's suffering becomes symptom for that which does not speak (hysteric discourse). All this discussion of purloined authority is another way of saying that when woman speaks, her letter is purloined by patriarchal culture and diverted into the symptoms of, that is the suffering from, lack of discourse. As we have discovered, the purloined letter, lack of name, lack of saying becomes the central issue in *The Wanderer*.

Evelina's letter, purloined by Willoughby, signifies the usurpation of her discourse. If a letter is purloined, it must have therefore a proper course. Not only does the holder of the letter eventually come to be identified as its author, but also Man as the authority over, the possessor of, Woman comes to be identified as the author of woman. Insofar as the letter (woman) crosses the path of others, it determines *them* in their actions. "Man" is determined by his very determination to hold and conceal her as woman.

Willoughby's response signals how legitimate discourse identifies the female. Woman's letter, her description of herself, is concealed by the one who, in holding her letter, hides her manifold possibilities.[4] Willoughby diverts the letter but cannot prevent it from finding its proper course, cannot conceal the manifold possibilities of Evelina from shining forth, cannot stay the uncertainty of her possible revelations. Nor can he prevent Orville's discovery of Evelina's "capacity" and her understanding of Orville's integrity. Nonetheless, the purloined letter—held in sufferance as a cipher (Nobody)—does arrive at its destination: it reveals her because the condition of namelessness can no longer conceal her.

Foucault says, perhaps with questionable historical accuracy, that tradition does not ascribe the "rational entity" we call a historic, individual author until the late eighteenth century.[5] If a woman cannot claim to be the "rational entity" we call an author, or if, as in the cases of Burney, Evelina, and Camilla, she disavows her claim of authority over her letter(s), to whom then does the purloined letter belong? The letter as sign has no intrinsic meaning in itself but takes on meaning only through the intersubjective relations among senders, receivers and holders. As Burney's *Diary* has shown us, the letter functions as a communal pact or bond belonging to no one individual, and therefore, belonging to nobody. The letter's very existence sets in motion a symbolic chain of relationships. Whoever comes in contact with the letter is enmeshed in this web and, once again, those who wish authoritatively to name woman radically alter themselves instead. When a woman names, that is writes and *functions* as a (nonoriginary) author, her letter finds its destination not only in spite of, but by the very fact that its authority suffers this diversion. Those who come in contact with the wanderer are enmeshed in a similar context of relationships that discloses them as they try to uncover her identity. Narrating her (nameless) condition names the who that is "unnamed, unknown without any sort of recommendation," the who that is called woman.

Evelina writes a narrative about her namelessness: her particular condition and that of woman in general. She is protected in her transgressive act of authorship not only by common standards governing letters but also because Burney "edits" the letters and allows for the fiction that they were not meant for critical, public scrutiny. Burney in turn displaces her own "transgression," as she calls it. She undercuts her own narrative authority by acknowledging woman's *real* condition: "Without name, without recommendation, and unknown," another version of "Nobody." This address is repeated in some form in each of her novels, subverting the concept of subjectivity that has dominated Western thought. In repeatedly addressing "Nobody" in her works, Burney refuses to call upon the legislating consciousness of patriarchy that had produced her condition and ask it to minister to its victims. She refuses patriarchal authority in saying that "concealment is the only boon I claim."

Revelation *in* concealment—the two occur together to form the relationship between namelessness and name. While in fact writing a narrative about Evelina writing a narrative about herself, Burney places herself in the "peculiar situation of the editor," who, "though trembling for their [the letters'] success from a consciousness of their imperfections, yet fears not being involved in their disgrace, while happily wrapped up in a mantle of impenetrable obscurity" (original preface). In this way she ameliorates her transgression by denying her own authority; Evelina does the same. "I cannot write the scene that followed," she insists, and then writes it. Burney is a transgressor when she uses authoritative discourse in the process of disclaiming it; she speaks across the grain of her time while speaking from within its texture. Even while paying allegiance to the standard that names her "woman," she transforms it, opens up another possibility for woman, in Kristeva's words, "to give a language to the intrasubjective and corporeal experiences left mute by culture."[6] This saying, this process of naming, creates a new category for thought, changing the very discourse that sustains the world of those who named her and revealing that name depends on both the said and the unsaid. In Burney's works, language and name come into a new relationship that shifts the ground upon which legitimate discourse stood.

Recall that Evelina needed a legitimate name in the sense of rank or recognition in order to merit a name in marriage. She does not, like a bastard, require the legitimacy of authenticated birth; instead she needs public acknowledgment of her actual legitimacy so that she can find a place in the social order and no longer be a no one.[7] Evelina *is* like a bastard, however, in that she is someone of dubious or spurious origin, resembling, but not truly of, the ranking species: Man. In other words, she needs to have her name legitimated by the community as having truth value because she cannot legitimate it herself. In his foreword to Lyotard's *The Postmodern Condition*, Fredric Jameson says that representation is an "essentially realistic epistemology" that reproduces for subjectivity, "an objectivity that lies outside it . . . whose fundamental evaluative categories are those of adequacy, accuracy, and Truth itself" (viii). In other words, "the rule of consensus" for approving the truth value of statements depends on the legitimacy of language; if, for example, a statement is "cast in terms of a possible unanimity between two rational minds: this is the Enlightenment narrative."[8] If woman has no right to the rational mind of the Enlightenment narrative, her name has no legitimacy; her statements lack interpretive force and cannot be included in the prevailing discourse for consideration by the community. This is the problem of legitimacy for Evelina and one that forces her to write and name, and thus authenticate, her own narrative.

Lyotard distinguishes between two kinds of knowledge, "scientific" and "narrative," the former held to be authentic and the latter inauthentic. Those unverifiable fables and myths, other strange medleys of thoughts and facts fit for women and children, actually shape significant human life. The "strange medley" is not the veridical data of nature; it is the stuff of human vision within which veridical data arises.

Ironically, Evelina convinces her father of her right to his name, not by way of rational argument or a pathetic appeal to justice, but by means of her visible resemblance to her mother. This form of truth, written in her face and form and written in Evelina's narrative, alters the conceptual ground upon which the *nom de pere* stands. Belmont exclaims upon seeing her, "My God! does Caroline Evelyn still live! . . . thou image of my long lost Caroline!" (*Evelina*, 354). Confronted with Evelina's physical presence, the shape of John Belmont's *own* narrative is suddenly transformed. He is altered even further when his narrative history is recounted by Caroline Evelyn's letter. In other words, he accounts for Evelina (and thus, recounts himself) by means of a proof that takes the form of narrative.

On that account, the legitimacy of Evelina's surname rests upon narrative; her name is not limited to actual speech, and not determined by scientific proof (documents, the prior appeals of others, the confession of the nurse, etc.). Since narratives define what has the right to be said and who has the right to say it, since they are themselves a part of culture, they constitute ordinary social practices. Hence Evelina's legitimacy actually rests upon her *lack* of legitimate discourse as narrated in her letters and not upon the model of intellectual reasoning that assumes authority over discourse. Existential namelessness allows her name to be disclosed and gives to us a singularly distinct woman.

We now need to rethink how Cecilia acquiesces to the name "Delvile" in the light of this dismantling of patriarchal authority. The plot turns on the clause in the will of Cecilia's uncle by which her future husband must take her name or forfeit her fortune. Cecilia does eventually renounce her fortune in marrying Delvile, "thus portionless, though an heiress," and as a result, the family name, "on loan" to her, reverts to a distant cousin.

"Renounce" belongs to the verb *to forgive*: to excuse for a fault, to remit an offense and free the offender, to pass over without demanding justice. By renouncing her name, Cecilia, like Burney, gives up a claim to the rule of name over woman. That is, Cecilia renounces holding name in her possession as her uncle thought he could do "by his arbitrary will, as if an ordinance of his own could arrest the course of nature! and as if *he* had power to keep alive by the loan of a name, a family in the male branch already extinct" (462). Without releasing the Delviles from the consequences of what they, as representatives of the patriarchal rule of name represent, Cecilia and her capacity to act would, as it were, be confined to one single deed from which she could never recover. She would always remain merely a passive victim. Cecilia reveals herself, her "name" in the act of renouncing her name, becoming "nobody." She redeems herself when she shows us that "lack of name and past" *is* her past, *is* her name.

Cecilia's madness, like Camilla's rejection of the pen of iron, renounces the consciousness that would use the discourse of the other (irrationality) as an occasion to assert itself in what is for her the most horrifying of realities. She renounces any reassertion of self-consciousness. Renunciation releases, both accommodates and looses, the past. It gives to Cecilia a historical—not mimetic—identity. This identity is *always* provisional because it depends on the configuration of multiple relationships in continual flux. Nonetheless, this contextual being, a triumphantly de-objectified no-thing, is also grounded in her particular historical circumstances.

Though the "woman" created by the patriarchy has neither access nor right to the "discourse of the father" because of explicit and implied prescriptions, "she" fits that powerless role and, paradoxically, enables such discourse to exist in the first place. Far from merely opposing this negating identity, Burney reappropriates the woman that the patriarchy obscures. As we have seen in *The Wanderer*, the revelatory character of "namelessness" redeems Juliet's "female difficulties" and names her "indefinable, unconquerable, unfathomable Incognita!" (4:163).

In the light of such a renunciation of patriarchy, to demand that Burney's work fit the conventions of the novel, or to invent from the conventions an agenda for female resistance, returns Burney to the legislating practices of authorial power. Rather, releasing the literary work from its autonomy celebrates the name-invoking process of language as an activity in Nobody's tradition.

Burney's Nobodies can be viewed as flat nothings, understood only through the creation of a set of emotional, nearly incoherent outpourings, or they can be seen as a history of Woman that even in its concealment opens a more promising potential for women. This view sees the concept *woman* as a process of *both* revelation *and* concealment. Producing women conversationally emphasizes process, not telos but open-endedness. To demand that Nobody be congruous with a defined female somebody implies seeing human character as a substantial entity; it privileges the already-said rather than the possibly-sayable. Lack of discourse from the perspective of Nobody discovers the preconceptual power of language in women's lived experience. From out of her own lived odyssey, Burney, like Odysseus with the Cyclops, exploits the special powers of going nameless.

The very excessiveness of suffering depicted in these narratives— chance meetings, misguided letters, flights into danger, madness, sickness, hysteria, attests to the unspeakable power of language. Foucault calls these functions a "too-muchness" of a "wave-like succession to infinity . . . to approach always closer to the moment where language will reveal its absolute power."[9] In other words, at its limits mere speech breaks off and language manifests its revelatory power. Woman's namelessness marks the discourse that Irigaray calls "female," one that avoids rigid definitions and metaphors that stabilize, and most of all one that avoids the illusion of authority over language.

These narratives tell us more about woman if we remember that the author, Frances Burney, is another fictional narrative. At best we can isolate various female agents in these narratives, but we can never say their stories are complete. Narrating namelessness says that the unsayable woman is a mode of language, of speaking, and of being heard. The power of these narratives, especially *The Wanderer*, in a postmodern world derives neither from acquiescing to woman's condition nor rebelling against it. As thinker of a woman's condition, Burney reflects attentively on the understanding that is opened up from within the heart of the life of her age. She does not ask us to quit thinking Woman as nameless absence, as mere negativity, but to think her more fully, more radically. The culture that demands a female be Nobody has given Burney to herself, has given us the opportunity to rethink our cultural narrative. Burney's own story as "Nobody" celebrates what Kristeva describes as "the multiplicity of every person's possible identifications . . . the relativity of his/her symbolic as well as biological existence."[10]

In conclusion, there is a paradigm for this world that is our destiny in Burney's writings. She dedicated herself to "journalizing" from the time of her early teens until the time of her death at the age of eighty-two. When writing her father's memoirs, she "felt herself to be the guardian of her father's fame, and no more tender guardian could have been found or fancied." Even in old age, Burney considered herself from the light of her father's gaze. Certainly woman has shaped herself from the image the father's culture held up to her. Yet, her absence from the ruling discourse of the father guards the revolutionary power of language itself, that potentiality reserved for the poet. The poet, by imaginatively inhabiting a limiting identity, Nobody as "nobody very important," "nothing but a body," explores the potential of that identity and makes it limitless.

Since Burney at one time served as her father's copier, she treated the memoirs of her family's correspondence like sacred texts in need of preservation. Traditionally, the sacred writing of texts was an act of discipline, compassion, and devotion: discipline, because one must remain true to the character of the text in the sacred act of passing it on; compassion, as a move to hold the sacred values alive for future generations; devotion, as the combination of the other two. Not only did the copied text pass on the body of culture it preserved, it bore the gestures of the nobody who copied it and inscribed the copier in the process:

> To every signifying mark, every tracing of thought which appears on the surface of the original text, there corresponds a gesture— the gesture, namely, which produced it.[11]

Hannah Arendt says that "the human essence can come to be after someone departs leaving only a story" (*HC*, 238). For Burney, writing what only in death came to be her life, copying the history of her generation's correspondence was a similarly sacred act. Likewise in her novels, every signifying mark of the written text has a corresponding silent gesture marking the person who produced it, so that both marks, the written and the unwritten, become her, that is, woman's, history.

In the letter Edmund Burke wrote to Burney in which he effusively praises *Cecilia*, he captures the appreciation of the age for both her work and her modesty: "In an age distinguished by producing extraordinary women, I hardly dare to tell you where my opinion would place you amongst them. I respect your modesty, that will not endure the commendations which your merit forces from everybody."[12] It is in "the grace, the balance, the measure" of Nobody, who in modesty merely wished to keep alive for future generations what others accomplished, that this extraordinary woman shines forth. More than marks upon a page, her writing speaks from and to silence, from what has been forgotten to what we may again forget; from what has been overlooked to what has not yet been said; from the realm of the concealed unspoken to the abiding space of revelation. There, in the space of human possibility, we find the question asked of every "nobody" as a newcomer to the world: "Who are you?"

Notes

Introduction

1. One form of the juvenile diary can be found in *The Early Journals and Letters of Fanny Burney* 1768–1773, 1:1–2. Since Burney gave herself no fixed identity, no single authoritative name, readers are now faced with three possible ways of referring to her. (1) We can preserve the diminutive and intimate "Fanny" as the name favored by tradition and the early diary where she also calls herself "Nobody" and "friend." (2) We may, in hoping to restore dignity to female authorship and in opposition to common practice, call her "Frances Burney," after the title page of *Cecilia*. (3) We can defer to the title pages of *Camilla* and *The Wanderer*, where she inscribes herself "by the author of [the earlier novels]" with dedications signed by "F. d'Arblay" and "F. B. d'Arblay" respectively. Because the issue of name and the question of authority are central to this discussion, I call her "Fanny Burney" out of respect for her plurality and the wish not to energize patriarchy by either opposing it or by using her married name.

2. Barbara Johnson explains Jacques Derrida's critique of Western metaphysics in this excerpt from her introduction to Derrida's *Dissemination*, viii.

3. From the original dedication to *Evelina*, unpaginated.

4. Julia L. Epstein, "Fanny Burney's Epistolary Voices," 162. Epstein develops the issue of voice and silence in *The Iron Pen: Frances Burney and the Politics of Women's Writing*.

5. As Mary Poovey reminds us in "Feminism and Deconstruction," 51.

6. Luce Irigaray links the feminine with the fluid, plural, multi-voiced rather than with the singular, fixed, and univocal. She reflects that "our horizon

will never stop expanding; we are always open . . . we have so many voices to invent in order to express all of us everywhere, even in our gaps . . ." (*This Sex Which Is Not One*, 213. All further references cited within the text as *TSNO*).

1. *Evelina:* Writing Between Experience and Innocence

1. Fanny Burney, *Evelina* (New York: Norton, 1965). All subsequent quotations from this edition will be cited within the text. Richard Burney, Fanny's cousin, was himself puzzled with Evelina's simple character and Lord Orville's unaccountable politeness.

2. T. B. Macaulay, "Review of *Diary and Letters of Madame D'Arblay,*" 569. Macaulay further claims that "the very name novel was held in horror among religious people" and that even the circulating library was considered diabolical. Burney's feat was to be able to show the fashionable life of London and yet placate the codes of morality.

3. *The Early Diary of Frances Burney:* 1768-1778, ed. Annie Raine Ellis (London: George Bell, 1913), 2:237.

4. Macaulay and *The Journals and Letters of Fanny Burney,* ed. Joyce Hemlow. See also Joyce Hemlow's *The History of Fanny Burney,* for an account of Burney's reception by the reviewers.

5. Rose Marie Cutting, "A Wreath for Fanny Burney's Last Novel: *The Wanderer*'s Contribution to Women's Studies," 80.

6. *Early Diary,* 2:217 (1778).

7. Edward A. Bloom, ed. *Evelina,* introduction, xix. J.M.S. Tompkins, *The Popular Novel in England,* 1700-1800, in her chapter, "The Female Novelists," argued that "prudence is essentially self-government in the interests of the community, and it is well to use ourselves to this liberal interpretation of the word in dealing with the ethics of the women writers and with their ideal of womanhood" (141). Katharine M. Rogers, *Feminism in Eighteenth-Century England,* cites Evelina as an example of enforced passivity because she is forbidden to take any initiative to encourage Orville or discover his sentiments (164). See Hemlow, "Fanny Burney and the Courtesy Books," 759, and Mary Poovey, *The Proper Lady and the Woman Writer.* Poovey notes that the situation and behavior of the proper lady is constitutive of her and, on that account, prolongs her innocence. The moral virtues of the proper lady are accomplishments acquired without a learned intelligence and thereby indicative of woman's nature. These virtues are paradoxical in that they are innate and yet need constant vigilance and cultivation. The conduct books mirror the values and rhetorical strategies that conceptualize a woman (16).

8. While it is of great sociological interest to say that females were oppressed by the constraints of men, it is important to remember that in the prevailing

theoretical discussions of the term *patriarchal,* the father function is not limited
by gender. The patriarchy is the entire Western locus of authority and origin
under question here. In contrast, "Female innocence, then, is male oppression."
Patricia Meyer Spacks, "'Ev'ry Woman Is at Heart a Rake,'" 31. See also
Spacks's *The Female Imagination.* In "Archimedes and the Paradox of Feminist
Criticism," in *Feminist Theory: A Critique of Ideology,* Keohane et al., eds., 189–
215, Myra Jehlen proposes that "impotent feminine sensibility" is a basic structure of the novel (214). She also sees interiority as metaphorically female; since
the novel demands interiority, the hero who is sensitive is repeatedly described
in feminine terms; consequently, the "interior self" represented in novels is the
"female interior self in all men" (212).

9. The notion of character as a permanent, stable, psychological subject or
as a similar literary or linguistic entity has been challenged on many fronts:
Lacan, Kristeva, Irigaray, Kofman in psychoanalysis; Heidegger, Derrida, Foucault in philosophy; Habermas, MacIntyre, Arendt in political theory; Rorty
in ethics; Bakhtin, Lukács, J. M. Bernstein in literary theory of the novel;
Kuhn and Richard Bernstein in science, to name a few. Foucault summarizes
this entitative subject as the "author-function" which is "tied to the legal and
institutional systems that circumscribe, determine, and articulate the realm of
discourses." See Michel Foucault, "What is an Author?" *Language, Counter-
memory, Practice,* 130.

10. Julia L. Epstein's "Fanny Burney's Epistolary Voices" and *The Iron Pen*
(93–122) account for how Evelina thwarts the language of suppression. Though
the notion of epistolary voice in this essay may seem similar to that of Epstein,
I use voice in terms of an intersubjectivity without origin and not as multiple
versions of one voice.

11. John J. Richetti says that as a narrator, Evelina reveals "linguistic su-
periority" more than an "impressionable and fanciful sentimental heroine."
"Voice and Gender in Eighteenth-century Fiction: Haywood to Burney," 269.
To say that Evelina interprets is to say that she is a hermeneut.

12. Catherine Parke distinguishes between the "I" who cannot simultaneously note itself and write and the "Name" signifying the "functional counterpart of the third person" and "appearance in a world of appearances," in
"Vision and Revision: A Model for Reading the Eighteenth-Century Novel of
Education," 165.

13. Mary Wollstonecraft, *A Vindication of the Rights of Woman,* says that men
have developed ingenius arguments to prove that the two sexes acquire character
by different means: "Women are not allowed to have sufficient strength of mind
to acquire what really deserves the name of virtue." Furthermore, women are
"kept in ignorance under the specious name of innocence." She continues, "In
fact, it is a farce to call any being virtuous whose virtues do not result from
the exercise of its own reason." She adds, "Purity of mind . . . is something

nobler than innocence, it is the delicacy of reflections, and not the coyness of ignorance" (122, 123).

14. Kristina Straub sees *Evelina* as a patriarchal book divided against itself and the eighteenth-century model for the female as a decline into powerlessness in *Divided Fictions: Fanny Burney and Feminine Strategy* and also in "Women's Pastimes and the Ambiguity of Female Self-Identification in Fanny Burney's *Evelina*," and "Fanny Burney's *Evelina* and the 'Gulphs, Pits, and Precipices' of Eighteenth-Century Female Life."

15. For an overview of how modern theorists see name, naming, and name-ability as symptomatic of the problem of language and subjectivity see Chris Weedon's *Feminist Practice & Post-Structuralist Theory,* chap. 4.

16. In using terms like *commodity* and *bourgeois economy* I wish to acknowledge the force of Marxist critique of quantification, reified persons, and social relations, without taking materialist theory as the basis for my argument about this novel, or making a specifically economic argument. Evelina's lack of wealth and name are not simply material conditions; her situation in life is *already interpreted* in cultural discourse. An a priori interpreted discourse is her material condition. Hence my position is a hermeneutic one. For a social critique of *Evelina* see Judith Lowder Newton in *Women, Power & Subversion: Social Strategies in British Fiction, 1778–1860,* 23–54, 50.

17. For a description of Burney's use of irony and comedy in this novel see Margaret Anne Doody, *Frances Burney: The Life in the Works.*

18. Jacques Lacan, "Seminar on 'The Purloined Letter.'" Theft, according to the Promethean myth, makes the one who steals it feel he is a god, in control, author of the word. Patriarchal authoring fails to signify difference, here the female unsaid. Lacan labels the unsaid as the other or the desire of the other mediated by linguistic modes. It is through the desire (lack) of the other that man's desire finds form, enlanguaged because language is the displacement of desire, the Derridean textuality where the perpetual restructuring of the subject takes place. Any construct of woman will always be subverted by other discourses that exceed it.

19. Luce Irigaray relates the concept of woman to women's suffering (neurosis) and woman's lack of discourse in *This Sex Which is Not One.* The publisher's notes on Irigaray's key terms are especially helpful here (219–22). See also Sarah Kofman, *The Enigma of Woman: Woman in Freud's Writings,* on Freud's positing of woman's narcissism and hysteria.

20. Naomi Schor follows the history of the patriarchal censure of the detail, the excessive, or the particular in her *Reading in Detail: Aesthetics and the Feminine.*

21. See "Richardson's Sources," in Cynthia Griffin Wolff's *Samuel Richardson and the Eighteenth-Century Puritan Character,* 14–58. Terry Eagleton's discussion of the epistolary in *The Rape of Clarissa* is based on Wolff's work.

22. See Margaret Doody's comments on the decorum of the epistle in her introduction to *Pamela.*

23. For the "sendings" of letters as the play of alterity or différance see Jacques Derrida's *The Post Card,* and in particular "Le Facteur de la Vérité" (413-96) on Lacan and Poe.

24. The following is Dr. Burney's account of his response to *Evelina* and especially to the character of Villars:

> I opened the first volume with fear and trembling; not having the least idea that, without the use of the press, or any practical knowledge of the world, she could write a book worth reading. The dedication to myself, however, brought tears into my eyes; and before I had read half the first volume I was much surprised, and, I confess, delighted; and most especially with the letters of Mr. Villars. She had always had a great affection for me; had an excellent heart, and a natural simplicity and probity about her that wanted no teaching.

From a letter included in Fanny Burney's *Memoirs of Dr. Burney,* 1:169, 170.

25. Kathleen B. Jones, "On Authority: Or, Why Women Are Not Entitled to Speak," in *Feminism & Foucault,* ed. Irene Diamond and Lee Quinby, 119-33.

26. Jean-François Lyotard and Jean-Loup Thebaud, *The Postmodern Condition: A Report on Knowledge,* 6-9.

27. On the binary axis of public-private, self-world, etc., see Straub's *Divided Fictions,* and Katherine Rogers, "Fanny Burney: The Private Self and the Published Self."

28. "Woman Can Never be Defined," in *New French Feminisms,* ed. Elaine Marks and Isabelle de Courtivron, 137.

2. *Cecilia:* The Madness of Reason

1. Frances Burney, *Cecilia* (London: George Bell, 1882), 52. All further citations, including volume, noted in the text.

2. Annie Raine Ellis cites this issue in the preface to *Cecilia,* (vii-viii).

3. Hester Thrale, *Thraliana: The Diary of Mrs. Hester Lynch Thrale 1776-1809,* 536.

4. Simone de Beauvoir, *The Second Sex,* 480.

5. *Madness and Civilization,* ix-x. Hereafter referred to in the text as *MC.* Foucauldian feminists would caution us that when Foucault displaces Man, he does not account for his own position when he re-naturalizes woman. See *Feminism & Foucault.* Biddy Martin's essay, "Feminism, Criticism, and Foucault," 3-20, describes this issue.

6. Barbara Hill Rigney, *Madness and Sexual Politics in the Feminist Novel,* preface.

7. John Mullan, *Sentiment and Sociability: The Language of Feeling in the Eighteenth Century.* Mullan refers to the medical texts of the eighteenth century in describing hypochondria, hysteria, and madness as the last refuge for the moral and pure (16, 201-40).

8. Alice A. Jardine, *Gynesis: Configurations of Woman and Modernity.*

9. Julia Kristeva calls the language of representation (scientism) male and "symbolic," and the language of feminine discourse poetic or "semiotic," in *Revolution in Poetic Language* (cited in the text as *Revolution*).

10. Sandra M. Gilbert and Susan Gubar, *The Madwoman in the Attic,* 22, 78. Gilbert and Gubar claim that female authors project nonconforming impulses onto their "mad" creations, enabling the female to come to terms with her feelings of division (22). Kristina Straub (*Divided Fictions*) follows up this argument by assigning a sexual motive to Cecilia's madness. Cecilia, afraid of Delvile, sees a bloody vision of marriage and responds by dissociating herself from male versions of communicative action. Madness is Cecilia's most effective moment of communication because she controls the men who have power over her.

11. Hannah Arendt links speech to action in *The Human Condition.* See chap. 5, "Action," 175-244. All further references will be cited in the text as *HC*.

12. Patricia Spacks, *Imagining a Self,* 181.

13. Kristeva elaborates this point in her chapters "Negativity: Rejection" and "Heterogeneity" in *Revolution.* She discusses madness in "Practice" and notes (as Ricoeur does in talking about Freud's "semantics of desire") that Freud's notion of repression already partakes of language so that, properly speaking, the repressed cannot be outside language and therefore cannot be repressed. Poetic language (for example, Cecilia's madness) does not express "symptoms of the neurotic ego idealizing the repressed" but instead expresses "*a modification of linguistic and logical linearity and ideality* [*sic*], which cannot be located in any ego" (164).

14. Margaret Doody, *Frances Burney: The Life in the Works,* 119.

15. Martin Heidegger, "Letter on Humanism," in *Basic Writings,* 225.

3. *Camilla:* The Heart Has Its Reasons

1. *Camilla* (Oxford: Oxford University Press, 1983), 483. All further references cited in the text.

2. Samuel Johnson, "Idler 57," in *Works of Samuel Johnson,* 2: 176.

3. Edward A. Bloom and Lillian D. Bloom, introduction to *Camilla* by Frances Burney, xvi.

4. Margaret Doody, *Frances Burney: The Life in the Works,* xvii. Doody suggests that the novel is a domestic epic (240) and cites the noneconomic, domestic factors that influenced *Camilla*'s composition. Elsewhere she says it is concerned with creating a language that is nonrational and social (262).

5. Katharine M. Rogers, *Feminism in Eighteenth-Century England,* 120.

6. Rose Marie Cutting, "Defiant Women," 520, 521. Meriting the pleasure of her lover is such an arduous and contradictory task, Cutting adds, that the hapless Camilla "faces difficulties that could drive any woman into paranoia." Spacks suggests that women at that time were encouraged by the expectations of men to display a highly susceptible sensitivity, especially when exhibiting softness, delicacy, and timidity (*Imagining a Self,* 182, 183).

7. For the sake of her place in culture, the female "overlooks problems, excuses faults, and suppresses anger" (Larry Blum et al., "Altruism and Women's Oppression," 241).

8. Poovey, tracing the development of the proper lady during the seventeenth and eighteenth centuries, notes the standard of propriety applied to both female authors and their female characters; accordingly, she sees Camilla as "struggling to master the conventions of female indirection" (25). J.M.S. Tompkins observes that although the proper attitude for the early female author-heroine was "diffidence," and although her contribution to literature was a mere indulgence by men, the male public generally—perhaps wistfully—expected from the female novelists "a glimpse into the ideal world of sensibility and melting affection that they hoped was inhabited by their womankind" (125).

9. Poovey, 16–23.

10. Nancy K. Miller, "Emphasis Added: Plots and Plausibilities in Women's Fiction."

11. Terry Eagleton, *The Rape of Clarissa,* 79.

12. Teresa de Lauretis, *Alice Doesn't,* 9.

13. As Seyla Benhabib and Drucilla Cornell point out in *Feminism as Critique: On the Politics of Gender,* such oppositions are the effects of "dominant Western conceptions [*read* patriarchal] of reason and rationality" and "multi-gendered, intersubjective relations" that "leave traces in every gendered subject," 15, 117. This collection of essays, written by women in philosophy, law, sociology, and political science, questions the following theories: Marx's fundamental premises, "power" politics, communitarian and Frankfurt school versions of praxis, categories of social life, feminist and other versions of "the unencumbered self," unreconstructed versions of the female subject, all forms of psychoanalysis. Much of my discussion is in agreement with theirs.

14. Arendt, *HC.* See her section, "The Rise of the Cartesian Doubt," 273–79.

15. "Desire becomes bound up with the desire of the Other, but that in this loop lies the desire to know," Jacques Lacan, *Écrits,* 301.

16. Jane Gallop, *Reading Lacan*, translates this as, "Desire is knotted to the desire of the Other, but . . . in that loop lies the desire to know" (184). She says that "the subject wants the real Other to calm her desire, wants the ideal Other to be blind to desire, because the subject's desire is inextricably knotted up with the Other's desire" (184). Stuart Schneiderman's paraphrase is this: "Desire is always the desire of the Other . . . because desire always seeks recognition by the Other's desire." He says, "Those who wish to create a society in which Otherness is nonexistent, come to be alienated from their own desire." *Jacques Lacan: The Death of an Intellectual Hero*, 174. See Lacan, *The Four Fundamental Concepts of Psycho-Analysis*, "The Field of the Other and Back to the Transference," 216–30.

17. Gallop, 152.

18. Hans-Georg Gadamer, *Truth and Method*, 217.

19. J. M. Bernstein, in *Philosophy of the Novel*, analyzes Descartes's *Discourse on Method* as the ur-novel grounding the "self" as form (157–65). Catharine MacKinnon, "Feminism, Marxism, Method, and the State," in *Feminist Theory: A Critique of Ideology*, ed. Keohane et al., quotes John Berger's *Ways of Seeing* in describing the objectified female. Edgar says of Camilla: "She knows she has not only her own innocence to guard, but the honor of her husband. Whether she is happy with him or not, this deposit is equally sacred."

20. From Hannah Arendt's "The Concept of History," in *Between Past and Future*, 61.

21. Arendt, "Concept," 61.

22. Jacques Derrida, *Spurs: Nietzsche's Styles*, 109.

23. Julia Epstein, *The Iron Pen*, cites the pen as a patriarchal instrument of violence that Camilla domesticates (150).

24. Heidegger, "Letter on Humanism," in *Basic Writings*, 228.

25. Josef Pieper, *Leisure: The Basis of Culture*, 90–103, 98.

4. *The Wanderer:* Naming Woman

1. A traditional response to Burney's last novel charges that *The Wanderer* is "a book which no judicious friend to her memory will attempt to draw from the oblivion into which it has justly fallen." T. B. Macaulay's criticism, written during the decade following its publication in 1814 (in which only 3,600 copies were sold), is still often repeated. "Review of *Diary and Letters of Madame D'Arblay*." For the history of critical response to Burney's works see Epstein, *Iron Pen*.

2. Luce Irigaray, *This Sex Which Is Not One*, 122, 123.

3. *Propre, nom propre, propriété, approprier* are a cluster of related words connecting for Luce Irigaray the notions of capitalism and patriarchy: "Demand

for order . . . the proper name, and the proper or literal meaning of a word, on the one hand, and the concepts of property ownership and appropriation on the other." *Propre* is one of those French adjectives (like *grand*) which changes meaning with position. Placed after the noun, it means neat, or specific, but placed before the noun, it means *own*. Irigaray's wordplay says that one's first, given, or Christian name is one's own proper name, as opposed to the family's proper name. See publisher's note on selected terms (*TSNO,* 221).

4. Though she describes Juliet's namelessness as a radical political move on Burney's part (*Iron Pen,* 178), Epstein sees Elinor as speaking for Juliet's resentment (188).

5. Much of the major critical work on *The Wanderer* focuses on its description of "female difficulties," and we owe a great debt to the critics who see the social and economic dilemma of women in the two main female characters. Rose Marie Cutting talks about Juliet's "trap of dependency" ("Defiant Women," 521). Patricia Spacks advances the view that "goodness amounts to Juliet's only viable resource" and claims that the novel expresses Burney's deep anger at woman's lot (*Imagining a Self,* 188). Mary Poovey (*Proper Lady*) expands this critical horizon by connecting the strategies of indirection employed by female writers and their female creations to the ideological prohibitions pervading society and, hence, pervading the literary-critical enterprise. In other words the ambagious indirections a female writer must employ in order to communicate her own view emerge in stylistic traits such as the episodic plot, sentimental outpourings, Gothic sensationalism, and discursiveness of the heroine's action and speech. In turn, all these traits are tied to cultural (ideological) prohibitions against women.

6. To restate this crucial matter in Mary Poovey's terms, if ideological (and therefore cultural) prohibitions bear upon the perspective in which this novel is viewed, then perhaps we need to better understand the concepts underlying the notion of ideology and culture (*Proper Lady,* 43).

7. Katherine Rogers suggests that real security for women can only come from Elinor's kind of assertiveness along with a certain disregard for propriety; she hastens to add, however, that Juliet redefines courage through "secret reasoning and cool calculation of consequences" (*Feminism,* 220). On the same premise, Cutting attempts to redeem Burney from the canon of conservative female authors by describing *The Wanderer,* and especially Elinor, as early champions of feminism. Margaret Doody lauds Elinor's "theatricality," adding that her "sensibility" and her "capacities for both protest and self-destruction" are parallels to Burney's own life (*Life in the Works,* 342).

8. Julia Kristeva, "Woman Can Never Be Defined," Marks & de Courtivron, eds. *New French Feminisms,* 137–41.

9. Frances Burney, *The Wanderer,* 5 vols. (London: Longman, Hurst, et al., 1814), 1:73. All further references cited with volume number in the text.

10. Benhabib and Cornell (*Feminism as Critique*) criticize the "generalized other" in their introduction.

11. Schneiderman, *Jacques Lacan,* 113–16. The bleeding woman's uterine hemorrhage could have been stopped by a physician, but the cure would have addressed only the symptom and blocked the significance of the bleeding. Concerning the analyst's power to disclose the meaning of the symptoms, it is well to keep in mind a precautionary note from Jane Gallop which questions the analyst's ability to interpret the neurotic. This power can only be "illusory" (*Reading Lacan,* 29).

12. Georg Lukács, *History and Class Consciousness,* in his chapter on "Reification and the Consciousness of the Proletariat," gives us the seminal definition of reification.

13. "Women and Literature in the Eighteenth Century," 55.

14. Arendt sees narrativity as the political praxis constituting a world (*HC,* 186). Other versions of her theory of narrativity are as follows: Lukács, *Theory of the Novel;* J. M. Bernstein, *The Philosophy of the Novel;* Jean-François Lyotard, *The Postmodern Condition;* Richard J. Bernstein, *Philosophical Profiles: Essays in a Pragmatic Mode;* Fred R. Dallmayr, *Polis and Praxis: Exercises in Contemporary Political Theory*—to name just a few.

15. John Keats, *Selected Poems and Letters,* ed. Douglas Bush (Boston: Houghton Mifflin, 1959), 261. This is from a description of Negative Capability in a letter, 21 or 27 December 1817.

16. P. L. Heath, "Concept," *The Encyclopedia of Philosophy,* 2:176.

17. See William M. Sullivan, *Reconstructing Public Philosophy,* 164, 202–3. Sullivan argues that most modern and postmodern forms of political praxis are based upon some form of the social contract. Arendt comments on the social contract in "What is Authority," in *Between Past and Future,* 99.

18. Janet Todd, *Women's Friendship in Literature,* 318.

19. George Steiner, "Literature and Post History," in *Language and Silence,* 388.

20. J. M. Bernstein claims that Lukács's *Theory of the Novel* is a political narration of the fate and meaning of narrative in our time (267). The novel asks us about another historical subject who can narrate beyond the aesthetic, or literary, domain by offering us a past and a narrative to come.

21. Arendt describes the power of promise as concomitant with freedom (*HC,* 244, 245).

22. Arendt, *On Revolution,* 97.

23. Frances Burney, *Journals and Letters,* 2 October 1792.

24. Wollstonecraft, *Vindication,* 14.

5. 'Nobody' Is the Author

1. All references to the early diary are within the body of this chapter with the following documentation: those references from *The Early Journals and Letters*

of Fanny Burney, volume 1, ed. Lars E. Troide (Oxford: Clarendon, 1988), are listed by volume, page, and date. *The Early Diary of Frances Burney: 1768–1778,* 2 vols. ed., Annie Raine Ellis (London: George Bell, 1913), is cited as *ED* with volume, page, and date.

2. Michel Foucault, "What is an Author?" in *Language, Counter-Memory, Practice,* 125, cited in this chapter as Foucault.

3. Arendt describes otherness or difference as the "curious quality of *alteritas* possessed by everything that is" (*HC,* 176).

4. The difficult problem of just what constitutes a work such as the *Diary* can best be described in Foucault's words:

> Assuming that we are dealing with an author, is everything he wrote and said, everything he left behind, to be included in his work? This problem is both theoretical and practical. . . . But what if, in a notebook filled with aphorisms, we find a reference, a reminder of an appointment, an address or a laundry bill, should this be included in his works? Why not? These practical considerations are endless once we consider how a work can be extracted from the millions of traces left by an individual after his death. (118–19)

Thus, we have multiple versions of the Burney journals and letters. The multivolumed *Journals and Letters of Fanny Burney, 1791–1840* (Oxford: Clarendon, 1972) 1–12 consists of the "residue" left from Fanny's own vigorous editing.

5. "Inconsistent" is the earlier version of what Troide edits as "insolent" in the early diary.

6. Jacques Derrida, *Positions,* more than anyone else, has goaded us into an awareness of the power in language, both its impulse to mastery, logocentrism, and its impulse to mystery, *différance.* This power does not belong to the author, nor does she control, authorize, or initiate the play of différance (14).

7. Martin Heidegger, *Basic Problems in Phenomenology,* says that for the autonomous subject, every representing is an *I* represent, *I* judge, *I* will. The knowing subject is self-consciousness, the "I-am" that pits itself against all objects (126).

8. *The Famous Miss Burney,* ed. Barbara G. Schrank and David J. Supino (New York: John Day, 1976), a collection from the diaries and letters that includes excerpts beyond the 1778 date of the *Juvenile Diary,* cited in the text as *FMB* with page and date.

9. Foucault says that the notion of property and ownership in writing was established in the copyright laws of the late eighteenth century ("What Is an Author?" 125).

10. From a letter written by Daddy Crisp in which he quotes back to Fanny what she related to him as coming from Johnson (*FMB,* 100 [1778]).

6. Woman's Revelation and Women's Revolution

1. *Memoirs of Dr. Burney,* 124.

2. Toby A. Olshin, "To Whom I Most Belong." He claims that Evelina's difficulties are due neither to ignorance nor inexperience. It is Evelina's obscure birth and search for a "proper family" that occasions her difficulties (29). Evelina is judged because of her "incorrect familial context."

3. Mary Poovey, "Fathers and Daughters," 42.

4. Barbara Johnson, *The Critical Difference* (Baltimore: Johns Hopkins University Press, 1980), documents the famous quarrel between Derrida and Lacan in her chapter, "The Frame of Reference."

5. Foucault, "What Is an Author?" 124.

6. Julia Kristeva, "Woman's Time," in *The Kristeva Reader,* 194.

7. Olshin, 31. Foucault talks about narratives as "verbal clusters" which do not belong to the familiar categories of book and author ("What Is an Author?" 124–25).

8. Lyotard, *The Postmodern Condition,* sec. 6–9, 8–12.

9. Foucault, "Language to Infinity," in *Language, Counter-memory, Practice,* 65.

10. Kristeva, "Women's Time," 210.

11. David Michael Levin, *The Body's Recollection of Being,* 188.

12. Frances Burney, *The Famous Miss Burney,* 136.

A Selected Bibliography

Works by Frances (D'Arblay) Burney

Camilla. Edited by Edward A. Bloom and Lillian D. Bloom. Oxford: Oxford
   University Press, 1972.
Cecilia. 2 vols. London: George Bell, 1882.
Diary and Letters of Madame d'Arblay. 4 vols. Edited by Charlotte Barrett. London:
   George Bell, 1891.
The Early Diary of Frances Burney, 1768–1778. Edited by Annie Raine Ellis. 2 vols.
   London: George Bell, 1889.
The Early Journals and Letters of Fanny Burney: 1768–1773. Vol 1. Edited by Lars
   E. Troide. Oxford: Clarendon, 1988.
Evelina. New York: W. W. Norton, 1965.
The Famous Miss Burney. Edited by Barbara G. Schrank and David J. Supino.
   New York: John Day, 1976.
Journals and Letters of Fanny Burney, 1791–1840. Edited by Joyce Hemlow, et al. 12
   vols. Oxford: Clarendon, 1972.
Memoirs of Dr. Burney. 3 vols. London: Edward Moxon, 1832.
The Wanderer. 5 vols. London: Longman, Hurst, Rees, Orme, and Brown, 1814.

Secondary References

Abel, Elizabeth, ed. *Writing and Sexual Difference*. Chicago: University of Chicago
   Press, 1982.
Agonito, Rosemary. *History of Ideas on Woman*. New York: Perigee, 1977.

Arendt, Hannah. *Between Past and Future*. New York: Penguin, 1954.

———. *The Human Condition*. Chicago: University of Chicago Press, 1958.

———. *The Life of the Mind*. New York: Harcourt, 1971.

———. *Men in Dark Times*. New York: Harvest, 1955.

———. *On Revolution*. New York: Pelican, 1977.

Benhabib, Seyla, and Drucilla Cornell, eds. *Feminism as Critique*. Minneapolis: University of Minnesota Press, 1987.

Bernstein, J. M. *The Philosophy of the Novel: Lukács, Marxism and the Dialectics of Form*. Minneapolis: University of Minnesota Press, 1984.

Bernstein, Richard J. *Philosophical Profiles*. Philadelphia: University of Pennsylvania Press, 1986.

Brown, Martha G. "Fanny Burney's 'Feminism': Gender or Genre?" In *Fetter'd or Free?: British Women Novelists, 1670–1815*, edited by Mary Anne Schofield and Cecilia Macheski, 29–39. Athens: Ohio University Press, 1986.

Brownstein, Rachel M. *Becoming a Heroine*. New York: Penguin, 1984.

Bloom, Edward A., and Lillian D. Bloom. "Fanny Burney's Novels: The Retreat from Wonder." *Novel* 12 (1979): 215–35.

Bloom, Harold, ed. *Fanny Burney's "Evelina."* Modern Critical Interpretations. New York: Chelsea House, 1988.

Blum, Larry, et al. "Altruism and Women's Oppression." In *Women and Philosophy*. Edited by Carol C. Gould and Marx W. Wartofsky, 222–47. New York: Perigee, 1976.

Cutting, Rose Marie. "A Wreath for Fanny Burney's Last Novel." *Agora* 3 (1974): 80–91.

———. "Defiant Women: The Growth of Feminism in Fanny Burney's Novels." *Studies in English Literature* 17 (1977): 519–30.

Dallmayr, Fred R. *Polis and Praxis: Exercises in Contempory Political Theory*. Notre Dame: Notre Dame University Press, 1984.

de Beauvoir, Simone. *The Second Sex*. Translated by H. H. Parshley. New York: Vintage, 1952.

de Lauretis, Teresa. *Alice Doesn't*. Bloomington: Indiana University Press, 1984.

Descartes. *Philosophical Works*. Translated by Elizabeth S. Haldene and G. R. L. Ross. 2 vols. New York: Dover, 1955.

Derrida, Jacques. *Dissemination*. Edited by Barbara Johnson. Chicago: University of Chicago Press, 1981.

———. *Positions*. Translated by Alan Bass. Chicago: University of Chicago Press, 1982.

———. *The Post Card*. Translated by Alan Bass. Chicago: University of Chicago Press, 1987.

———. *Spurs: Nietszche's Styles*. Translated by Barbara Harlow. Chicago: University of Chicago Press, 1978.

———. *Writing and Difference*. Translated by Alan Bass. Chicago: University of Chicago Press, 1978.

Diamond, Irene, and Lee Quinby, eds. *Feminism & Foucault*. Boston: Northeastern University Press, 1988.

Doody, Margaret A. *Frances Burney: The Life in the Works*. New Brunswick: Rutgers University Press, 1988.

————. Introduction to *Pamela* by Samuel Richardson. Edited by Peter Sabor. New York: Penguin, 1980.

Du Plessis, Rachel Blau. *Writing Beyond the Ending: Narrative Strategies of Twentieth-Century Women Writers*. Bloomington: Indiana University Press, 1985.

Eagleton, Terry. *The Rape of Clarissa*. Minneapolis: University of Minnesota Press, 1982.

Epstein, Julia L. "Fanny Burney's Epistolary Voices." *Eighteenth Century* 27 (1986) 2:162–79.

————. *The Iron Pen: Frances Burney and the Politics of Women's Writing*. Madison: University of Wisconsin Press, 1989.

————. "Writing the Unspeakable: Fanny Burney's Mastectomy and the Fictive Body." *Representations* 16 (Fall 1986): 131–66.

Foucault, Michel. *The History of Sexuality*. Translated by Robert Hurley. New York: Vintage, 1980.

————. *Language, Counter-memory, Practice*. Translated by Donald F. Bouchard and Sherry Simon. Ithaca: Cornell University Press, 1977.

————. *Madness and Civilization*. Translated by Richard Howard. New York: Vintage, 1973.

————. *The Order of Things*. New York: Vintage, 1973.

Gadamer, Hans-Georg. *Truth and Method*. New York: Seabury, 1975.

Gallop, Jane. *Reading Lacan*. Ithaca: Cornell University Press, 1985.

Gerin, Winifred. *The Young Fanny Burney*. London: Thomas Nelson, 1961.

Gilbert, Sandra M., and Susan Gubar, eds. *The Madwoman in the Attic*. New Haven: Yale University Press, 1979.

Hale, Will Taliaferro. "Madame D'Arblay's Place in the Development of the English Novel." *Indiana University Studies* 3 (1916): 5–35.

Heath, P. L. "Concept." In *The Encyclopedia of Philosophy*, edited by Paul Edwards, 177–80. Vols. 1 and 2. 1967 ed.

Heidegger, Martin. *Martin Heidegger: Basic Writings*. Edited by David Farrell Krell. New York: Harper, 1977.

————. *Basic Problems in Phenomenology*. Translated by Albert Hofstadter, Rev. Ed. Bloomington: Indiana University Press, 1988.

————. *The End of Philosophy*. Translated by Joan Stambaugh. New York: Harper, 1973.

————. *On the Way to Language*. Translated by Peter D. Hertz. New York: Harper, 1971.

————. *Poetry, Language, Thought*. Translated by Albert Hofstadter. Harper, 1971.

Hemlow, Joyce. "Fanny Burney and the Courtesy Books." *PMLA* 65 (1950): 732–55.

————. *The History of Fanny Burney*. Oxford: Clarendon Press, 1958.

Irigaray, Luce. *This Sex Which Is Not One*. Translated by Catherine Porter. Ithaca: Cornell University Press, 1985.

Jacobus, Mary. *Reading Woman: Essays in Feminist Criticism*. New York: Columbia University Press, 1986.

Jardine, Alice A. *Gynesis: Configurations of Woman and Modernity*. Ithaca: Cornell University Press, 1985.

Johnson, Samuel. *Rasselas*. New York: Holt Rinehart, 1958.

————. *Works of Samuel Johnson*. Yale Edition. New Haven: Yale University Press, 1963.

Kauffman, Linda S. *Discourses of Desire: Gender, Genre, and Epistolary Fictions*. Ithaca: Cornell University Press, 1986.

Keohane, Nannerl O., et al., eds. *Feminist Theory: A Critique of Ideology*. Chicago: University of Chicago Press, 1981, 1982.

Kofman, Sarah. *The Enigma of Woman: Woman in Freud's Writing*. Translated by Catherine Porter. Ithaca: Cornell University Press, 1985.

Kristeva, Julia. *The Kristeva Reader*. Edited by Toril Moi. New York: Columbia University Press, 1986.

————. *Revolution in Poetic Language*. New York: Columbia University Press, 1984.

————. *Tel Quel*. Summer (1974): 165–67.

Lacan, Jacques. *Écrits*. Translated by Alan Sheridan. New York: W. W. Norton, 1977.

————. *The Four Fundamental Concepts of Psycho-Analysis*. Translated by Alan Sheridan. New York: W. W. Norton, 1978.

————. "Seminar on 'The Purloined Letter.'" *Yale French Studies* 48 (1972): 39–72.

Levin, David Michael. *The Body's Recollection of Being*. Boston: Routledge & Kegan Paul, 1985.

Lukács, Georg. *The Historical Novel*. Lincoln: University of Nebraska Press, 1962.

————. *History and Class Consciousness*. Translated by Rodney Livingstone. Cambridge: MIT Press, 1968.

————. *The Theory of the Novel*. Translated by Anna Bostock. Cambridge: MIT Press, 1971.

Lyotard, Jean-François, and Jean-Loup Thebaud. *Just Gaming*. Translated by Wlad Godzich. Minneapolis: University of Minnesota Press, 1985.

————. *The Postmodern Condition: A Report on Knowledge*. Translated by Geoff Bennington and Brian Massumi. Minneapolis: University of Minnesota Press, 1984.

Macaulay, T. B. "Review of *Diary and Letters of Madame D'Arblay*." *Edinburgh Review* 75 (January 1843): 523–70.

Marks, Elaine, and Isabelle de Courtivron, eds. *New French Feminisms: An Anthology*. New York: Schocken Books, 1981.

Miller, Nancy K. "Emphasis Added: Plots and Plausibilities in Women's Fiction." *PMLA* 96 (1981): 36–47.

———. "Women and Literature in the Eighteenth Century." *Women and Literature* 7 (1979): 52–56.

Mullan, John. *Sentiment and Sociability: The Language of Feeling in the Eighteenth Century.* Oxford: Clarendon, 1988.

Newton, Judith Lowder. *Women, Power and Subversion: Social Strategies in British Fiction, 1778–1860.* London: Methuen, 1985.

Olshin, Toby A. "To Whom I Most Belong." *Eighteenth-Century Life* 6 (October 1980): 29–42.

Parke, Catherine. "Vision and Revision: A Model for Reading the Eighteenth-Century Novel of Education." *Eighteenth-Century Studies* 16 (Winter 1982–1983) 2:162–74.

Pieper, Josef. *Leisure: The Basis of Culture.* New York: Pantheon, 1952.

Poovey, Mary. "Fathers and Daughters." In *Women and Literature,* edited by Janet Todd, 39–58. New York: Holmes & Meier, 1981.

———. "Feminism and Deconstruction." *Feminist Studies* 14 (Spring 1988): 51–65.

———. *The Proper Lady and the Woman Writer.* Chicago: University of Chicago Press, 1984.

Pratt, Annis, et al. *Archetypal Patterns in Women's Fiction.* Bloomington: Indiana University Press, 1981.

Ricoeur, Paul. *Freud and Philosophy.* Translated by Denis Savage. New Haven: Yale University Press, 1970.

———. *The Philosophy of Paul Ricoeur.* Edited by Charles E. Reagan and David Stewart. Boston: Beacon, 1978.

———. *The Rule of Metaphor.* Translated by Robert Czerny. Toronto: University of Toronto Press, 1975.

———. *Time and Narrative.* Vol. 1. Translated by Kathleen McLaughlin and David Pellauer. Chicago: University of Chicago Press, 1983.

Richetti, John J. "Voice and Gender in Eighteenth-century Fiction: Haywood to Burney." *Studies in the Novel* 19 (Fall 1987): 263–72.

Rigney, Barbara. *Madness and Sexual Politics in the Feminist Novel.* Madison: University of Wisconsin Press, 1978.

Rogers, Katharine M. *Before Their Time: Six Women Writers of the Eighteenth Century.* New York: Frederick Ungar, 1979.

———. *Feminism in Eighteenth-Century England.* Urbana: University of Illinois Press, 1982.

———. "Fanny Burney: The Private Self and the Published Self." *International Journal of Women's Studies* 7 (1984): 110–17.

———. *The Troublesome Helpmate: A History of Misogyny in Literature.* Seattle: University of Washington Press, 1966.

Russ, Joanna. *How to Suppress Women's Writing*. Austin: University of Texas Press, 1983.

Schneiderman, Stuart. *Jacques Lacan: The Death of an Intellectual Hero*. Cambridge: Harvard University Press, 1983.

Schor, Naomi. *Reading in Detail: Aesthetics and the Feminine*. New York: Methuen, 1987.

Showalter, Elaine, ed. *The New Feminist Criticism*. New York: Pantheon, 1985.

Spacks, Patricia Meyer. *The Female Imagination*. New York: Knopf, 1975.

———. *Gossip*. New York: Alfred A. Knopf, 1985.

———. *Imagining a Self*. Cambridge: Harvard University Press, 1976.

———. "'Ev'ry Woman Is at Heart a Rake'." *Eighteenth-Century Studies* 8 (1974): 27–46.

Spender, Dale. *Feminist Theorists: Three Centuries of Key Women Thinkers*. New York: Pantheon, 1983.

———. *Man Made Language*. London: Routledge & Kegan Paul, 1980.

Steiner, George. *Language and Silence: Essays on Language, Literature and the Inhuman*. New York: Atheneum, 1970.

Straub, Kristina. *Divided Fictions: Fanny Burney and Feminine Strategy*. Lexington: University Press of Kentucky, 1987.

———. "Fanny Burney's *Evelina* and the 'Gulphs, Pits, and Precipices' of Eighteenth-Century Female Life." *The Eighteenth Century: Theory and Interpretation* 27 (1986): 230–46.

———. "Women's Pastimes and the Ambiguity of Female Self-Identification in Fanny Burney's *Evelina*. *Eighteenth-Century Life* 10.2 (May 1986): 58–72.

Sullivan, William M. *Reconstructing Public Philosophy*. Berkeley: University of California Press, 1986.

Thrale, Hester. *Thraliana: The Diary of Mrs. Hester Lynch Thrale, 1776–1809*. Edited by Katherine C. Balderston. Oxford: Clarendon, 1951.

Todd, Janet. *Women's Friendship in Literature*. New York: Columbia University Press, 1980.

Tompkins, J.M.S. *The Popular Novel in England, 1770–1800*. Lincoln: University of Nebraska Press, 1961.

Watt, Ian. *The Rise of the Novel*. Harmondsworth: Penguin, 1972.

Weedon, Chris. *Feminist Practice and Post-Structuralist Theory*. London: Basil Blackwell, 1987.

Wolff, Cynthia Griffin. *Samuel Richardson and the Eighteenth-Century Puritan Character*. Hamden, Conn.: Archon Press, 1972.

Wollstonecraft, Mary. *A Vindication of the Rights of Woman*. Edited by Carol H. Poston. New York: W. W. Norton, 1975.

Young-Bruehl, Elisabeth. *Hannah Arendt: For Love of the World*. New Haven: Yale University Press, 1982.

Index

Action: definition of, 100–102; female, 50, 85; and relation to
promise, 100, 52–103 passim, 106–
7; vs. passivity, 85, 91, 94
—forms of: narrativity, 85, 89, 99;
political, 85, 99
Affectivity: definition of, in *Camilla*,
53–55, 58–59, 62, 65–67, 71, 74–75;
eighteenth-century, 55; feminine
virtue of, 36, 38, 49, 60; maintenance of, 39, 47, 49, 55; problem
of, 61; ruling passion of, 34–52,
106; as spontaneity, 67, 107; as
sympathy, 55; unnameable, 78;
vs. rationality, 31, 33–52, 53–81.
See also Female desire; Rationality; Sensibility; Sentiment
—display of: in *Camilla*, 31, 57–81; in
Cecilia, 31, 43–45, 48–50; in *Evelina*, 19–20
Alterity, female, 1, 153n.7; political
concept of, 100; unnamed feminine, 2
Arblay, France d'. *See* Burney,
Frances

Arblay, General Alexander d' (husband), 122
Arendt, Hannah, 7, 141, 153n.3; on
relation of speech and action,
148n.11
—description by: of common sense,
120; of empiricism, 69; of narrativity, 110, 152n.14
Author: autonomy of, 140; concept
of, in early diary (Burney), 109–
30 passim; concept of, in Foucault, 110, 130; as father-god, 124–
25; as female scribbling, 10, 33;
letters of, 13–31 passim, 105; as
Nobody, 109–30 passim; patriarchal, 20, 26, 33, 77, 80, 123–27; as
plurality, 27, 110, 119, 129–30; and
relation to authority, 24–27, 48,
77, 110, 119, 127. *See also* Early diary (Burney); individual works
Authority: female, 27, 127, 128; lack
of, 19–31, 48, 134; patriarchal, 20,
24, 26–28, 41, 77, 110, 128, 138; and
relation to authorship, 23–28, 33,
48, 77, 108–30 passim